# BAT BOY
## THE MUSICAL

STORY AND BOOK BY
**KEYTHE FARLEY**
AND **BRIAN FLEMMING**

MUSIC AND LYRICS BY
**LAURENCE O'KEEFE**

★

DRAMATISTS
PLAY SERVICE
INC.

BAT BOY: THE MUSICAL
Keythe Farley, Brian Flemming, Laurence O'Keefe

CAUTION: Professionals and amateurs are hereby warned that performance of BAT BOY: THE MUSICAL is subject to payment of a royalty. It is fully protected under the copyright laws of the United States of America, and of all countries covered by the International Copyright Union (including the Dominion of Canada and the rest of the British Commonwealth), and of all countries covered by the Pan-American Copyright Convention, the Universal Copyright Convention, the Berne Convention, and of all countries with which the United States has reciprocal copyright relations. All rights, including professional/amateur stage rights, motion picture, recitation, lecturing, public reading, radio broadcasting, television, video or sound recording, all other forms of mechanical or electronic reproduction, such as CD-ROM, CD-I, DVD, information storage and retrieval systems and photocopying, and the rights of translation into foreign languages, are strictly reserved. Particular emphasis is placed upon the matter of readings, permission for which must be secured from the Authors' agent in writing.

The English language stock and amateur stage performance rights in the United States, its territories, possessions and Canada for BAT BOY: THE MUSICAL are controlled exclusively by DRAMATISTS PLAY SERVICE, INC., 440 Park Avenue South, New York, NY 10016. No professional or nonprofessional performance of the Play may be given without obtaining in advance the written permission of DRAMATISTS PLAY SERVICE, INC., and paying the requisite fee.

Inquiries concerning all other rights should be addressed to International Creative Management, Inc., 40 West 57th Street, New York, NY 10019. Attn: Mitch Douglas.

### SPECIAL NOTE

Anyone receiving permission to produce BAT BOY: THE MUSICAL is required to give credit to the Authors as sole and exclusive Authors of the Play on the title page of all programs distributed in connection with performances of the Play and in all instances in which the title of the Play appears for purposes of advertising, publicizing or otherwise exploiting the Play and/or a production thereof. The names of the Authors must appear on separate lines, in which no other names appear, immediately beneath the title and in size of type equal to 50% of the size of the largest, most prominent letter used for the title of the Play. No person, firm or entity may receive credit larger or more prominent than that accorded the Authors. In addition, the credit for the *Weekly World News* must appear on a separate line, in which no other name appears, immediately beneath and in size of type equal to the names of the Authors. The billing must appear as follows:

BAT BOY: THE MUSICAL

Story and Book by
Keythe Farley and Brian Flemming

Music and Lyrics by
Laurence O'Keefe

Licensed Under Agreement with *Weekly World News*

The following acknowledgment must appear on the title page in all programs distributed in connection with performances of the Play in size of type equal to 25% of the size of the largest, most prominent letter used for the title of the Play:

2

Original New York production produced by Nancy Nagel Gibbs, Riot Entertainment, Robyn Goodman, Michael Alden, Jean Doumanian and The Producing Office.

Original cast recording available on RCA/Victor.

In addition, the following acknowledgment must appear within all programs distributed in connection with performances of the Play:

Bat Boy: The Musical was developed in New York City at The Directors Company, Michael Parva, Artistic/Producing Director.

Bat Boy: The Musical had its initial production at The Actors' Gang in Los Angeles, CA.

The authors wish to acknowledge the generous support provided through the Richard Rodgers Development Award and the Richard Rodgers Production Award. The Richard Rodgers Awards are administered by the American Academy of Arts and Letters.

# AUTHORS' NOTE

There are many ways to stage this show. A cast of ten is possible (see the New York credits), as is a cast of one hundred and ten. A spare set is fine; an elaborate set can work, too. Intense blood effects, no blood at all — it's up to your taste and your budget.

However, there is only one sure way to play this material — truthfully. BAT BOY is not a satire or a parody of musicals, though it presents skewed versions of familiar themes. And while BAT BOY is certainly meant to be enormous fun for the audience, to make that fun happen the artists interpreting the work must approach it with the same dedication and commitment they would apply to any tragedy. We have seen some interpretations of BAT BOY fail utterly because the interpreters chose to have too much of their own fun with it, or took a "metatheatrical" approach — a term we don't fully understand but apparently means the actors stand outside the material and comment on it — or tried to cram in too many of their own jokes, pratfalls and other silliness.

We've learned this the hard way: There is enough within this script and score to keep you busy. Adding too many extra bits or "metatheatrics" — again, we don't really know what that is, but you shouldn't do it — will undermine your performance and diminish the audience's enjoyment of the play.

These characters do not know they're funny. Their desires and fears are a matter of life or death to them. Please, never nudge the audience in the ribs or wink at them; the audience prefers to decide for themselves whether to laugh or cry. If you play these characters sincerely and truthfully and to the hilt, you'll get plenty of laughs, and you'll get much more.

> *Keythe Farley*
> *Brian Flemming*
> *Laurence O'Keefe*

BAT BOY: THE MUSICAL was first produced by Mitch Watson at the Actors' Gang El Centro Theater in Los Angeles, California, on October 31, 1997. It was directed by Keythe Farley; the choreography was by Derick LaSalla; the set design was by Evan Bartoletti; the lighting design was by David F. Hahn; the sound design was by Adam Philius; the costume design was by Jennifer K. Diebold; the make-up and special effects were by David Rockello; and the production stage manager was Robin Veith. The cast was as follows:

BAT BOY ....................................................................... Deven May
MEREDITH PARKER ............................................... Kaitlin Hopkins
DR. THOMAS PARKER ................................................ Chris Wells
SHELLEY PARKER ........................................................ Ann Closs
SHERIFF REYNOLDS ..................................................... Don Luce
RICK TAYLOR ............................................................ Gary Kelley
RON TAYLOR, PAN ........................................ John Michael Morgan
RANDI TAYLOR, LORRAINE ............................... Julie Ann Taylor
MAGGIE ............................................................. Elizabeth Tobias
NED .......................................................................... Ken Elliot
DAISY ............................................................... Greta Rose Bart
BUD ................................................................... Ray Hesselink

BAT BOY: THE MUSICAL was produced in New York by Nancy Nagel Gibbs, Riot Entertainment, Robyn Goodman, Michael Alden, Jean Doumanian and The Producing Office at the Union Square Theater on March 21, 2001. It was directed by Scott Schwartz; the musical director was Alex Lacamoire; the musical staging was by Christopher Gatelli; the set design was by Richard Hoover and Bryan Johnson; the lighting design was by Howell Binkley; the sound was by Sunil Rajan; the costume design was by Fabio Toblini; the hair and makeup were by Ann Closs-Farley; and the production stage manager was Renee Lutz. The cast was as follows:

BAT BOY ....................................................................... Deven May
MEREDITH PARKER ............................................... Kaitlin Hopkins
DR. THOMAS PARKER ............................................. Sean McCourt
SHELLEY PARKER ...................................................... Kerry Butler
SHERIFF REYNOLDS ................................................ Richard Pruitt
RICK TAYLOR, LORRAINE, DOCTOR, MR. DILLON .......... Doug Storm
RON TAYLOR, MAGGIE, CLEM ................................... Kathy Brier
RUTHIE TAYLOR, NED ..................................... Daria Hardeman
MRS. TAYLOR, ROY,
REV. BILLY HIGHTOWER, INSTITUTE MAN ......... Trent Armand Kendall
BUD, DAISY, PAN ......................................................... Jim Price

# CHARACTERS

BAT BOY
MEREDITH PARKER, wife
DR. THOMAS PARKER, husband
SHELLEY PARKER, their daughter

The Townsfolk:

SHERIFF REYNOLDS
RICK, RON AND RUTHIE TAYLOR, three teenage spelunkers
MRS. TAYLOR, their mother
LORRAINE, a rancher's wife
MAGGIE, senior representative, Hope Falls Town Council
DAISY, a schoolteacher
MR. DILLON, a rancher
BUD, a rancher
NED, a rancher
ROY, a townsman
CLEM, a townsman
REVEREND BILLY HIGHTOWER
PAN
VARIOUS ANIMALS
YOUNG MEREDITH
MEREDITH'S FATHER
MEREDITH'S MOTHER
A DOCTOR
INSTITUTE MAN

CHORUS: singers/dancers, additional townsfolk

# PLACE

The setting is Hope Falls, West Virginia. Population 500.

# TIME

The present.

# BAT BOY

## THE MUSICAL

### ACT ONE

#### Scene 1

*A cave. In darkness, the sound of running water. Out of the darkness
comes the voice of Bat Boy, singing.*

BAT BOY. *(Offstage.)* Oo-oo-oo-oo-oo. *(His melodious nonsense syllables rever-
berate off each other. He harmonizes with his own echoed voice. Then, from above:
Three spotlights pierce the darkness. The spotlights come from the miner's helmets of
Rick, Ron and Ruthie, who descend into the cave on rappelling ropes. All three are
awestruck. They pan their spotlights across the audience.)*

RICK. Whoa … Look at this.

RUTHIE. We've never been this deep before.

RON. What's that smell?

RICK. I don't know. But this cave rocks.

RUTHIE and RON. Fully.

RON. Are we gonna run out of rope?

RICK. *(Landing on stage.)* Nope. We have *got* to celebrate going deeper than any
human being has gone before. *(Ruthie and Rick land, too.)*

RUTHIE. Where are we, Rick?

RICK. That was a major vertical. This could be virgin territory.

RON. C-c-can we go back up now?

RUTHIE. *(Looking over downstage edge.)* It keeps going. Straight down!

RICK. This is a total scoop.

RUTHIE. All right, who's packing?

RICK. Reading my mind. *(Rick produces a small, serviceable bong. Rick and
Ruthie turn off their lights and spark up while Ron explores his surroundings. The
light on his head and the occasional sparking of the lighter are the only lights on stage.
Suddenly Ron's helmet-light crosses the face of Bat Boy. Bat Boy screeches.)*

RON. *(Turning away.)* Sweet Jesus!

RICK. What?

RON. *(Turning light back again to a blank cave wall.)* The cave monster!! The cave monster!!

RICK. Shut up, Ron.

RON. I saw him, Rick! I swear.

RUTHIE. There's no such thing as a cave monster, Ron.

RICK. *(Approaching Ron, mocking him.)* Ooh! It's the cave monster, Ron! The scary caaaave monster! *(Ron finds Bat Boy again with his light and points hysterically; finally, Rick looks.)* Whoa! *(Rick and Ruthie turn their lights back on. All three spelunkers scramble. The helmet-lights flash around everywhere.)*

RUTHIE. What?

RICK. It was over there. But then I turned back and ...

RUTHIE. Ahhhh! Over here! *(Bat Boy scurries about the stage and the spelunkers chase after him. Occasionally lights cross Bat Boy's body or the back of his head, but the audience never sees Bat Boy's face. Eventually, the spelunkers have Bat Boy caught in the glare of their helmet-lights. His back is to the audience and he is frozen with fear. He slowly backs up toward the downstage ledge. He is naked.)*

RON. What is it?

RUTHIE. It's some deformed kid.

RICK. It's a Bat Boy. It's okay, little guy. I'm Rick Taylor. This is my brother Ron. And this is my sister Ruthie.

RUTHIE. Can you say "Ruthie"?

RON. Shut up, Ruthie!

RICK. We are totally keeping this thing.

RON. We won't hurt you.

RICK. Take my hand. Come on.

RON. Don't be afraid. It looks scared.

RUTHIE. See if it likes Fritos. *(Produces some and offers them to Bat Boy.)* Fritos. See? Fritos. *(Bat Boy attacks Ruthie.)* AAAAAHHHHHH! *(Ron and Rick jump on top of Bat Boy and pummel him.)* I'm bit! I'm bit!

RON. Ruthie's bit! Ruthie's bit!

RICK. Get him, Ron!

RON. I'm getting him! *(Ron pulls Bat Boy off of Ruthie and pins him to the ground.)*

RUTHIE. Oh, mama! I don't wanna die!

RICK. You freakin' animal! *(Rick leaps up and stomps Bat Boy on the head.)*

## "HOLD ME, BAT BOY"
### (Company)


MAN #1.
  IN A CAVE MANY MILES TO THE SOUTH
  LIVES A BOY BORN WITH FANGS IN HIS
  MOUTH.
  SLEEPING UNTIL THE FADING LIGHT,
  FLYING THROUGH BLOODY DREAMS;
  WHEN HE AWAKES THE SUMMER NIGHT
  IS FILLED WITH SCREAMS.
WOMAN #1 and WOMAN #2.
  YOU HAVE HEARD HE WAS BORN IN THE BOGS.
  THAT HE FEEDS ON THE FLIES AND THE FROGS.
MAN #2.
  YOU CALL HIM "BEAST" OR "CHANGELING";
MAN #3.
  OR "DEMON CHIMPANZEE";
MAN #4.
  BUT WE WILL PROVE HE'S NO SUCH THING:
FOUR MEN, TWO WOMEN.
  HE'S MUCH LIKE ME!
(MAN #1, WOMAN #3 and WOMAN #4 join in.)
ALL NINE.
  AND ME!
  OH,
  HOLD ME, BAT BOY,
  TOUCH ME, BAT BOY,
  HELP ME THROUGH THE NIGHT.
  LOVE ME, BAT BOY,
  SAVE ME, BAT BOY,
  MAKE IT ALL TURN OUT ALL RIGHT!
MAN #2.
  HE WAS DRAGGED FROM HIS HOME,
  AND THROWN DOWN
  AT THE EDGE OF A COAL MINING TOWN.

MAN #5.

    THEY STRIPPED HIM OF HIS DIGNITY,

MAN #1.

    THEY BEAT HIM LIKE A GONG.

MAN #3.

    AND HE WAS KICKED REPEATEDLY,

ALL NINE.

    AND THAT WAS WRONG!

    SO WRONG!

| ALL but WOMAN #3. | WOMAN #3. |
|---|---|
| OH, HOLD THE BAT BOY, | WON'T YOU HOLD HIM! |
| TOUCH THE BAT BOY, | WON'T YOU TOUCH HIM! |
| | |
| BRING HIM TO THE LIGHT … | |
| | BRING HIM TO THE LIGHT! |
| LOVE THE BAT BOY, | WON'T YOU LOVE HIM! |
| SAVE THE BAT BOY, | SOMEONE SAVE HIM! |

ALL NINE.

    MAKE IT ALL TURN OUT ALL RIGHT!

*(Rick and Ron wheel on a wagon which carries a wriggling burlap sack with a hand sticking out of the top.)*

SHERIFF. You say it's the Bat Boy?

RICK. Yeah! It bit Ruthie.

RON. She's in the hospital.

RICK. It's huge.

RON. And it's fast.

RICK. And it hates Fritos. You gotta lock it up, Sheriff.

RON. And make it stand trial! *(Kicks the bag. Bat Boy squeals.)*

SHERIFF. Now boys! You go on and look after your sister, I'll take care of this Bat Boy.

MEN #2 and #3, WOMEN #1, #2 and #3.

    WOULD NO ONE DEFEND HIM,

    PROTECT HIM, BEFRIEND HIM,

    WOULD NONE HEAR HIS CRY?

WOMAN #3.

    YEAH, WOULD NONE HEAR HIS CRY, Y'ALL?

*(Sheriff leads the wagon past Bud, Clem and Mr. Dillon. The men get closer and closer to the bag during the scene.)*

DILLON.  You say you got the Bat Boy in that bag?

CLEM.  Dang!

BUD.  Whatcha gonna do with it, Sheriff?

SHERIFF.  I figure I'll just take it up to Dr. Parker.

CLEM.  I'll bet that's one powerful critter.

BUD.  I knew those stories were true.

DILLON.  You think Dr. Parker can handle a Bat Boy?

SHERIFF.  It can't be that difficult. The Taylor kids managed to capture him all by themselves.

BUD.  But they're all hopped up on dope. That's like fighting six people!

SHERIFF.  Dr. Parker's a good veterinarian, I'm sure he'll just put it down with no trouble. *(Bag wriggles.)*

ALL except SHERIFF.  Aaaah! Sweet wounded Jesus!

SHERIFF.  So long, boys.

MEN #2 and #3, WOMEN #1, #2 and #3.
   OR WOULD THEY DETEST HIM,
   ARREST HIM, MOLEST HIM?

WOMEN #1 AND #2.
   OR JUST LET HIM DIE?

MEN #2 and #3, WOMEN #1, #2 and #3.
   YOU CAN'T JUST STAND BY!

*(Maggie, Lorraine and Daisy. Sheriff walks by with wagon.)*

LORRAINE.  You say you got the Bat Boy in that bag?

DAISY.  What are you going to do with it?

SHERIFF.  I'm headed to Dr. Parker's.

LORRAINE.  He's gonna put it down, right?

MAGGIE.  That seems like a waste of resources. He might be useful around town.

LORRAINE.  Maybe we could train him to rustle up the cows — like a sheepdog.

DAISY.  Do we own it?

MAGGIE.  Sure we do. You know, we could put him on display and charge admission.

LORRAINE.  People would pay good money to see a Bat Boy. We could be the next Branson.

DAISY.  Can we see it?

LORRAINE.  Let's have a little peek, Sheriff.

SHERIFF.  All right. *(Opens bag a little; ladies peek.)*

ALL except SHERIFF.  Aaah! Sweet wounded Jesus!

SHERIFF.  Good day, ladies.

WOMAN #4.

YOU CAN'T LET HIM DIE!

ALL NINE.

YOU CAN'T JUST STAND BY!

MAN #5.

HE HAS SUFFERED, AND NOW IT'S YOUR TURN.

YOU ARE HERE NOT TO LAUGH, BUT TO LEARN.

WOMAN #4.

LISTEN TO HIS UNGODLY SHRIEK,

WATCH WHAT THEY PUT HIM THROUGH.

WOMAN #4 and MAN #5.

HEED THE TALE OF A FILTHY FREAK —

ALL NINE.

WHO'S JUST LIKE YOU!

… AND *YOU!*

AND YOU!

OH …

2 MEN, 2 WOMEN.

HOLD ME BAT BOY,

TOUCH ME BAT BOY,

WON'T YOU HELP ME
THROUGH THE NIGHT,
MAKE IT ALL TURN OUT
ALL RIGHT!
LOVE ME BAT BOY,

SAVE ME BAT BOY,

I'VE BEEN CALLING
OUT YOUR NAME,
COME AND TAKE AWAY
MY SHAME!

HOLD ME BAT BOY,

TOUCH ME BAT BOY,

3 MEN, 2 WOMEN

HOLD ME BAT BOY,

TOUCH ME BAT BOY,

MAKE IT ALL TURN OUT
ALL RIGHT!

LOVE ME BAT BOY,

SAVE ME BAT BOY,

COME AND TAKE AWAY
MY SHAME!

HOLD ME BAT BOY,

TOUCH ME BAT BOY,

YOU HEAR ME CRY
WHEN NO ONE HEARS,
WON'T YOU LICK AWAY               WON'T YOU LICK AWAY
MY TEARS;                         MY TEARS;
LOVE ME BAT BOY,

                                  LOVE ME BAT BOY,
SAVE ME BAT BOY,

                                  SAVE ME BAT BOY,
SINK YOUR FANGS
INTO MY SOUL,

                                  ONLY YOU CAN
                                  MAKE ME
                                  WHOLE!

ALL.
  HOLD ME BAT BOY,
  TOUCH ME BAT BOY,
  HOLD ME IN YOUR ARMS TONIGHT!


## Scene 2


*Parker home — living room. Meredith and Shelley clean the living room.*


SHELLEY.  Can I call Rick again?

MEREDITH.  That doesn't make sense, honey. You just left him a message an hour ago.

SHELLEY.  I know. But I want to find out if he's coming.

MEREDITH.  He'll think about you more if he talks to you less.

SHELLEY.  Mom, Rick already knows that I like him.

MEREDITH.  Don't talk like a slut, Shelley.

SHELLEY.  Sorry.

MEREDITH.  *(Crosses to Shelley; puts her arm around her.)* Courting is a slippery slope, dear, and it's a young lady's job to provide the friction. When I was your age a young lady didn't even call a boy, especially if she wanted to. If Rick is worthy of you, he'll know that he needs to call you back. Clean the railing.

SHELLEY.  But it's not dirty.

MEREDITH.  You can't wait until it *gets* dirty. You have to look out for these boys, Shelley. Most of them are so out of control with their ... hormones that they really aren't in charge of their actions. But you don't suffer from their hormonal problems, so you'll bear the responsibility if something ... happens.

SHELLEY.  Like what?

MEREDITH.  The wages of sin is death, sweetheart, that's all I'm saying. *(There is an authoritative knock at the door, accompanied by the sounds of a commotion.)*

SHERIFF.  *(Offstage.)* It's Sheriff Reynolds, Meredith! *(Meredith opens the door. Immediately, the Sheriff enters, holding onto Bat Boy, who is hooded and handcuffed and struggles nonstop to get away from the Sheriff. Bat Boy's hood has written on it: "Bites.")*

### "CHRISTIAN CHARITY"
*(Sheriff, Shelley, Meredith)*

SHERIFF.
  EVENING FOLKS!

                      SHELLEY.
                        WHATCHA GOT?

  DOCTOR HOME?

                      MEREDITH.
                        NO, HE'S NOT.

  WHEN'S HE BACK?

                        AN HOUR OR SO.
                      SHELLEY.
                        THE HECK IS THAT?

  WELL, I DON'T KNOW.

                      MEREDITH.
                        WHAT IN THE WORLD?
                      SHELLEY.
                        WHERE DID YOU FIND?
                      MEREDITH.
                        WHAT IS HE DOING?
                      SHELLEY.
                        HE'S OUT OF HIS MIND!
                      MEREDITH.
                        IS HE IN PAIN?
                      SHELLEY.
                        IS HE INSANE?

SHERIFF.

　MAYBE AND POSSIBLY;

　LET ME EXPLAIN:

*(Bat Boy has broken away from the Sheriff and is running aimlessly about the room. The Sheriff pistol-whips Bat Boy, knocking him out.)*

MEREDITH and SHELLEY.　No!

SHERIFF.　Aw, heck. Maybe I shouldn't've done that. But that boy was hoppin' like a scalded dog.

MEREDITH.　Boy?

SHERIFF.　Maybe. Frankly, that's why I'm here. I figure maybe we need a veterinarian to sort this out. I'm hoping Dr. Parker will know what to do.

SHERIFF.

　I DIDN'T KNOW WHERE ELSE TO TAKE HIM.

SHELLEY.

*(Off Bat Boy's twitch.)*

　MOM!

MEREDITH.

　SHELLEY, QUIET!

SHERIFF.

　CAN'T GO TO JAIL, HE'S UNDERAGE.

SHELLEY.

*(Off another twitch.)*

　MOM!

MEREDITH.

　SHELLEY, QUIET!

SHERIFF.

　FOLKS UP AT THE MED SCHOOL,

　BET THEY'D CARVE HIM UP OR BAKE HIM,

　I'D SEND THE FBI A PAGE,

　BUT I DON'T THINK WE'RE AT THAT STAGE —

　SO: HERE HE IS FOLKS, HE'S ALL YOURS!

　COULDN'T LEAVE HIM OUT OF DOORS,

　CREEPIN' ON ALL FOURS.

　WE COULD ALWAYS SHOOT HIM,

　BUT THAT DON'T SEEM RIGHT TO ME,

　'N I CAN'T RID MYSELF O' MY CHRISTIAN CHARITY.

SHELLEY.　Can we see him?

MEREDITH.　Shelley, get away.

SHERIFF.　You listen to your mother, Shelley. You don't want to be near it if it

15

wakes up.

MEREDITH.  Is it an animal or a …

SHERIFF.  It bit one of the Taylor kids.

SHELLEY.  Rick?

SHERIFF.  No, Ruthie.

SHELLEY.  Oh.

SHERIFF.  She'll be all right.

MEREDITH.
   SHELLEY, DON'T STARE,
   SHELLEY, DON'T POKE.
   WHAT IS THIS, SHERIFF,
   SOME KIND OF SICK JOKE?

SHELLEY.
   MOM, HE'S SO GROSS,
   MOM, CAN HE STAY?

SHERIFF.
   SHEL, I WAS HOPIN' YOU'D SEE IT THAT WAY.
   I'M COMIN' UP FOR RE-ELECTION,

SHELLEY.
   MOM!

MEREDITH.
   SHELLEY, QUIET!

SHERIFF.
   I GOTTA BRING THIS THING TO HEEL.

SHELLEY.
   MOM!

MEREDITH.
   SHELLEY, QUIET!

SHERIFF.
   A BOY WITH HIS COMPLEXION'S
   GONNA MEET WITH SOME OBJECTIONS,
   'N I THINK I KNOW HOW FOLKS WILL FEEL
   ONCE THEY HEAR THIS "BAT CHILD" IS FOR REAL —

SHELLEY.  *(To Sheriff.)* It's a Bat Child? *(To Meredith.)* Mom, we gotta keep it.

SHERIFF.  They're just callin' it that, Shelley. I can't say I know that's what it is. That's for your father to decide.

MEREDITH.  All right, Sheriff. You've done the right thing coming to us. I'll take care of the boy for you.

SHERIFF.  Ah, that's great, Meredith. I can't thank you enough for the favor. Do you need anything? He can be pretty feisty.

MEREDITH.  We can manage, I'm sure.

SHERIFF.  You're certain?

MEREDITH.  Dr. Parker has some cages. I'm sure we can find one that works.

SHERIFF.  Right. That's what I figured.

| SHERIFF. | MEREDITH. | SHELLEY. |
|---|---|---|
| 'N IF HE TURNS | | |
| INTO A PAIN, | | |
| CALL ME, | | |
| I GOT STUN GUNS | | |
| AND A CHAIN! | WHOA! | |
| | | OH! |
| SO, HERE | | |
| HE IS FOLKS, | DON'T STARE, | MOM! … |
| HE'S ALL YOURS! | SHELLEY, | LOOK AT HIM! |
| | PLEASE DON'T POKE. | I KNOW BUT |
| COULDN'T LEAVE | | |
| HIM | DON'T TOUCH HIM, | MOM … |
| OUT OF DOORS, | | LOOK AT HIM; |
| CREEPIN' ON ALL | | |
| FOURS. | SHELLEY, | WHAT'S WRONG |
| | DON'T PROVOKE. | WITH HIM? |

SHERIFF.

WE MAY HAVE TO PUT HIM DOWN,

ALL THREE.

FOR NOW WE'LL WAIT AND SEE.

WE CAN'T RID OURSELVES OF OUR

CHRISTIAN CHARITY.

*(Bat Boy rouses and squirms.)*

| SHERIFF. | MEREDITH. | SHELLEY. |
|---|---|---|
| SO, HERE HE | | |
| IS FOLKS, | DON'T STARE, | MOM! … |
| HE'S ALL YOURS! | SHELLEY, | |
| | PLEASE DON'T POKE. | |
| COULDN'T LEAVE | | |
| HIM | DON'T TOUCH HIM, | MOOOOMMM! … |
| OUT OF DOORS, | | |
| CREEPIN' ON ALL | | |
| FOURS. | SHELLEY, | |
| | DON'T PROVOKE. | |

SHERIFF.
    THOSE THUNDERCLOUDS ARE CLOSING IN,
ALL THREE.
    WE CAN'T JUST LET HIM BE.
*(Sheriff exits, obviously glad to wash his hands of the situation. Meredith and Shelley look at the figure of Bat Boy on the floor.)*
    WE CAN'T RID OURSELVES OF OUR CHRISTIAN CHARITY.
    WE CAN'T RID OURSELVES OF OUR CHRISTIAN ... CHARITY!
SHELLEY.
*(Off bat boy's twitch.)*
    MOM!
MEREDITH.
    SHELLEY, QUIET.
*(Meredith pulls the hood off Bat Boy's head. Bat Boy screams. All lights blackout except for a pin spot on Bat Boy's face.)*


## Scene 3


*Lights come back up on the Parker living room. Bat Boy, still screaming, is now in a cage. Shelley stands next to the cage. Bat Boy shakes the bars, throws himself about the cage and generally makes a spectacle of himself. The shrieking is awful.*


SHELLEY. *(Hands over ears.)* Shut up! Shut up! *(Calling to offstage.)* Mom, he won't shut up! *(To Bat Boy.)* Shut up shut up shut up shut up shut up. SHUT. UP!!! *(Meredith enters with a whole, cooked chicken on a platter.)*
MEREDITH. Yelling at him won't help, sweetheart.
SHELLEY. He's being a pill.
MEREDITH. *(Placing chicken just inside Bat Boy's cage.)* He's probably just hungry.
SHELLEY. You're giving him our dinner?
MEREDITH. Don't be selfish, sweetie. *(To Bat Boy.)* Come on, it's okay. You need to eat. *(Bat Boy moves closer.)* Go on, go on. *(Bat Boy suddenly gets down on all fours and screams at the chicken. He appears to be trying to scare it out of his cage.)*
SHELLEY. Mom, why is he screaming at the chicken?! Mom, make him stop! Ugh! *(Meredith removes the chicken from the cage. Bat Boy stops screaming.)*

SHELLEY.
  SUCH AN UGLY BOY.

  LIKE A STINKY BONY RAT.

  I DIDN'T KNOW HE'D
  LOOK LIKE *THAT!*

  WELL, LOOK AT HIM.

MEREDITH.

  He's just different.

  You wanted to keep him.

  Shelley!

(Lightning flashes and thunder claps. Meredith and Shelley look up at the lights as they flash and dim. Bat Boy whimpers in his cage.)

MEREDITH.   It's going to be quite a storm. (Meredith takes out candles and lights them.)

SHELLEY.
  STUPID STARVING FREAK …

  DOESN'T HAVE THE
  SENSE TO EAT …

  DROPPING DEAD RIGHT
  AT MY FEET …

  JUST LOOK AT HIM …

MEREDITH.

  Shelley, that's not nice.

  We just haven't figured
  out what he needs —

  Shelley!

  (Tearing up.)
  He's just …
  tired.

(To Bat Boy.)
  THAT'S MY MOM.
  SEE, SHE CRIES
  EVERY TIME A STRAY
  DOG DIES.

  NO ONE CALLS;

  NO ONE CLAIMS;

  SO WE PUT THEM DOWN
  AND NEVER LEARN THEIR NAMES …

  Well, I feel bad for them.

  Sure they call …

  Sometimes …

MEREDITH. Well, we can name him, sweetheart. What would you like to call him?

SHELLEY. Bat Boy. You gotta eat something, Bat Boy.

MEREDITH. That's cruel, dear.

SHELLEY. That's what he looks like —

MEREDITH. — we're not calling him Bat Boy —

SHELLEY. — but that's what he looks like —

MEREDITH. *Shelley.*

SHELLEY. *(Beat.)* What do you want to call him?

MEREDITH. Perhaps Montgomery …

SHELLEY. How about Ugly?

MEREDITH. Or maybe Edgar. *(Calling.)* Ed-gar! …

BAT BOY. *(Looks at Meredith.)* Gggnnnnwwgwoooo?

MEREDITH. Look! He likes that name.

SHELLEY. *(Calling.)* Ug-ly! *(Bat Boy looks at Shelley.)* He likes Ugly better.

MEREDITH. Edgar it is! Well, I'm going to try to make something else for him. You stay away from the cage, sweetheart.

SHELLEY. Okay. *(Meredith exits. There is a loud knock at the door.)* Rick! *(Shelley goes to the door and opens it. Rick comes tearing into the living room.)*

RICK. Are you guys okay? I heard the Sheriff brought the Bat Boy over here and — *(Sees Bat Boy; points; mouth open in shock.)* He's still alive?! He's in your house?!

SHELLEY. It's okay, Rick. He's confined.

RICK. That cage'll never hold him! My sister's in the hospital with a big ol' … *(Indicates a neck wound.)* … I can't believe you have him in the house!

SHELLEY. Mom says we gotta keep him till Dad comes home.

RICK. Your dad's just going to kill it, right?

SHELLEY. *(Shrugging, "I don't know.")* Mm-mm-mm. So whatcha wanna do tonight?

RICK.

*(To Bat Boy, rapping loudly and whitely.)*

 HEY THERE LITTLE FREAK YOU REMEMBER ME?

 WE WERE NEVER INTRODUCED PROPERLY.

 HEY, YOU GONNA CRY?

 YOU DON'T LOOK SO TOUGH BY THE LIGHT OF DAY.

 BUT WE AIN'T GONNA MURDER YOU RIGHT AWAY.

 FIRST WE GONNA BUY

 YOU LOTS O' FANCY CLOTHES!

 AND MAKE YOU CLIP YOUR TOES!

 AND WATCH YOU WALK AROUND IN MAKEUP

AND PANTYHOSE!

SHELLEY.

*(Laughing, imitating Rick.)*
> WE GONNA TAKE YOU BACK
> OUT BY THE RAILROAD TRACK

RICK and SHELLEY.
> AND LEAVE YOUR BODY FOR THE DOGS AS A MIDNIGHT
> SNACK!

RICK.
> YOUR PAPA WAS A PIG!

SHELLEY.
> YOUR MAMA WAS A SNAKE!

RICK.
> WE'RE GONNA SNAP YOU LIKE A TWIG AND DUMP YOU IN
> THE LAKE!

SHELLEY.

*(Getting into it quite a bit.)*
> WE GONNA CHAIN YOUR ARM
> TO AN ATOMIC BOMB
> AND MAKE YOU TAKE YOUR GRANDMAMA TO THE SENIOR
> PROM!

*(Shelley makes "human beatbox" noises. Rick stares at her.)*
What?

RICK.  Dude, you are so hot. *(Grabbing Shelley, still addressing Bat Boy.)*
> BUT FIRST I'LL SHOW YOU WHAT I WANNA DO
> TONIGHT,
> I WANNA BOUNCE IT WIT MY CREW TONIGHT.
> WE'LL MAKE SWEET LOVE IN FRONT OF *YOU*
> TONIGHT!

SHELLEY.  *(Laughing, pushing him away.)* Ew!

RICK.
> UH HUH! UH HUH! UH HUH! UH HUH!

SHELLEY.

*(To Rick.)*
> YOU KNOW MY MOM IS RIGHT UPSTAIRS TONIGHT.

RICK.
> THAT CHICK IS FULLY UNAWARES TONIGHT.

SHELLEY.  *(Mouthing silently in disbelief.)* "Chick"? …

RICK.
> AND IF SHE CATCHES US, WHO CARES TONIGHT? …

SHELLEY. *(Smiling, charmed.)* Me? *(Rick leans in close.)*

| RICK. | SHELLEY. |
|---|---|
| UH HUH, UH HUH, | UH HUH, UH HUH … |

*(They are now singing into each others' mouths.)*

| UH HUH, UH HUH, | UH HUH, UH HUH … |

*(They make out. Bat Boy has been watching with growing intensity and now begins bouncing up and down on the bars of his cage and making eager noises.)*

BAT BOY.

A HA A HA A HA A HAH! A HA A HA A HA A HAH!

RICK. You freak! Can't you mind your own business, Bat Boy?

SHELLEY. Stay away from the cage.

RICK. What … you wanna bite me like you bit my sister? You want a piece of me? Huh, tough guy? *(Bat Boy suddenly jerks his head at Rick and screams. Rick is startled, falls flat on his butt and scampers away like a coward. Shelley tries not to laugh.)*

RICK. That little freak! Did you see that?

SHELLEY. I told you. *(Rick turns on Bat Boy.)*

| RICK. | SHELLEY. |
|---|---|
| WHY YOU TRYIN' TO STEP TO ME, LITTLE CREEP? ARE YOU THROWIN' DOWN WITH ME, LITTLE FREAK? WHATCHA GONNA DO? | |
| | Rick! |
| COME ON LITTLE COWARD, LET'S GET IT ON, I'M GONNA MAKE YOU WISH YOU WERE NEVER BORN! WHEN I'M THROUGH WITH YOU! I'LL SHOW YOU HOW I SPILL YOUR BRAIN TONIGHT! | |
| | Rick … |
| I'LL RUN YOU OVER LIKE A TRAIN TONIGHT! | Stop it! … |
| I'LL PUT YOU IN A WORLD O' PAIN TONIGHT! SO COME ON, COME ON, COME ON, COME ON! | Hey! |
| | MOM! |
| I SHOULDA BROUGHT MY | |

22

LOADED GUN TONIGHT!

                                Mom!

BUT STOMPIN' YOU WILL
BE MORE FUN TONIGHT!

                                Help!

YOU'RE GONNA PAY FOR
WHAT YOU DONE TONIGHT!
SO
*(Makes kung-fu noises.)*
  WOOO-EEEE-YAAAAAH!!!

                              Mom, Rick's being a pill!

*(Rick takes out a bowie knife.)*
  I'M TAKIN' OUT MY BOWIE
KNIFE TONIGHT!

                              Omigod …

I'M GONNA END YOUR
WORTHLESS LIFE TONIGHT!

                              Mom!

I'M MAKIN' YOU MY PRISON
WIFE TONIIIIIAAAAAAIIIIGHHHHT!
  *COME ON!!!*

*(Bat Boy flees and huddles in a corner of his cage, scared. Enter Meredith, wearing an oven mitt.)*

MEREDITH.  Rick Taylor! What do you think you're doing?

RICK.  Ahhh …

MEREDITH.  A poor defenseless boy. That's how you treat him? *(Points to the door with the oven mitt.)* Get out of my house!

RICK.  I'm sorry, Mrs. Parker.

MEREDITH.  Get out of my house!

RICK.  He started it. *(Meredith still points to the door. Rick looks to Shelley, who is kneeling next to the cage, looking at Bat Boy.)* Oh, man. *(Moving to the door, mumbling.)* I don't know what the big deal is. *(Yelling back.)* I guess I'll just go and see how my *sister's* doing, then! In the hospital! *(Rick exits. Meredith crosses to Shelley, who is now crying. Meredith kneels with Shelley and holds her.)*

SHELLEY.  Boys are horrible.

MEREDITH.  *(Strokes her head.)* Oh, sweetheart. *(Bat Boy falls to the floor and passes out. Thunder. Lights go out and stay out.)* Oh, there go the lights.

SHELLEY.  He doesn't look very good, Mom.

MEREDITH.  He's had a hard day, dear.

SHELLEY. You don't think he's going to die, do you?

MEREDITH. I don't know.

SHELLEY. I'm never going to get another pet, never.

MEREDITH. Shelley, why don't you go get ready for bed? I'll come tuck you in in a minute.

SHELLEY. All right. *(Shelley exits. Meredith lights candles. Bat Boy moans.)*


### "A HOME FOR YOU"
### *(Meredith, Bat Boy)*


MEREDITH.
POOR LITTLE PERSON WITH EYES SO SAD,
WHERE IN THE DARK DID THEY HIDE YOU?
WHAT HAVE YOU SEEN
THAT COULD TEACH YOU THAT HAUNTED STARE?
POOR LITTLE CREATURE, IT MAKES ME MAD
TO THINK OF THE CHILDHOOD DENIED YOU,
BUT GIVE ME A CHANCE
AND WE'LL MAKE IT ALL RIGHT, I SWEAR.

'CAUSE WE'RE NOT HERE TO HARM YOU
OR MAKE YOU FEEL ASHAMED.
YOU CAN MAKE MISTAKES HERE
AND YOU WON'T BE BLAMED.
SO SHOW US HOW TO HELP YOU,
AND IF WE PULL YOU THROUGH,
THEN WE WILL FIND A HOME FOR YOU.
*(Meredith slowly opens the door of the cage. Bat Boy cowers.)*

HOME IS A WORD THAT YOU SHOULD HAVE LEARNED.
HOME IS WHERE PEOPLE ACCEPT YOU.
PEOPLE WHO TREAT YOU WITH LOVE,
WHICH IS AWFULLY RARE.
FAMILY'S A PLACE WHERE YOUR TRUST IS EARNED
BY FOLKS WHO ARE HAPPY THEY KEPT YOU.
WE'LL FIND A FAMILY WHO WON'T LET YOU DOWN,

I SWEAR.
'CAUSE WE'RE NOT HERE TO HARM YOU, OR —

BAT BOY.
OO OO OO OO OO OO.

*(Bat Boy finishes the phrase in a mournful wordless singsong. Meredith is stunned. Finally she leans forward and sings:)*

MEREDITH.
OO OO OO OO OO OO?

*(Pause. Bat Boy meets her gaze for the first time.)*

BAT BOY.
... OO OO OO OO OO.

*(Together they harmonize, tentatively at first, then with growing confidence and complexity.)*

TOGETHER.
OO OO OO OO OO OO,
OO OO OO OO OO OO.
OO OO OO OO OO OO,

MEREDITH.
NO, WE'RE NOT HERE TO HARM YOU,
OR MAKE YOU FEEL ASHAMED,
YOU CAN MAKE MISTAKES HERE,
AND YOU WON'T BE BLAMED.
SO TEACH US HOW TO LOVE YOU,
AND ONCE THE NIGHT IS THROUGH,
THEN WE MAY HAVE
A HOME FOR YOU.
SO SHOW ME WHAT TO GIVE YOU,
SEE, LOOK, I MADE A STEW.

BAT BOY.
OO OO OO OO,
OO OO OO OO.
OO OO OO OO,
OO OO OO.
OO OO OO OO,
OO OO OO.

*(Meredith offers Bat Boy a spoonful of stew. He tastes it, grimaces, spits it out and retreats into a corner of the cage, gagging and spitting.)*

AND SOMEHOW, IF YOU MAKE IT THROUGH,
THEN THIS MIGHT BE
A HOME FOR YOU.

BAT BOY.
*(Weakly.)*
... OO OO OO OO OO.

*(Blackout.)*

# Scene 4

*Hope Falls Slaughterhouse. Maggie, Sheriff, Lorraine, Daisy, Bud, Ned, Roy.*

MAGGIE.  As the honorable mayor of Hope Falls, West Virginia, I hereby call this meeting of the Town Council to order. *(Gavel.)* Okey-doke. I want to thank you all for coming out in this storm tonight. So, let's get this meetin' going. First order of business.

DAISY.  *(Writing.)* Number One.

MAGGIE.  Lorraine, I believe you have a report for us from the Revival Committee.

LORRAINE.  That's right, Mayor Maggie, I do. I am pleased to confirm that the Reverend Billy Hightower *will* be bringing his Tent Revival Meeting and Barbecue to Hope Falls come spring.

CROWD.  *(Ad-lib.)* That's great. / Good job, Lorraine. / I can't wait.

LORRAINE.  And the Revival Committee has decided that we should put the Revival Tent behind the VFW Hall with the back of it facing west so the afternoon sun illuminates the cross. You see, Reverend Hightower has but this translucent vinyl cross on the back of the tent — like stained glass but vinyl? — and we just thought that the sun shining through there would synergize the spiritual aesthetic.

MAGGIE.  That's just great. Lorraine, that is excellent work. Okey-doke. Agenda Item Number Two.

DAISY.  Two.

MAGGIE.  Now the reason that I've called this Town Council meeting here in the slaughterhouse, is because we've got a crisis on our hands! I want you to take a look at these meat hooks. There's something peculiar about 'em, isn't there? There's no meat on 'em! Now we got three ranchers in attendance. Bud, Roy, Ned — let's have the report. How come this slaughterhouse ain't slaughterin'?

BUD.  Well, Mayor Maggie, that's a complicated question and it deserves a complicated answer. You see, the state of West Virginia has rules about how heavy a heifer's got to be in order that you can bring it to slaughter. And our cows just aren't up to the standard.

MAGGIE.  So what you're saying is that the cows are too skinny to kill.

NED.  Well, that's what the state regulations are saying. Me personally, I think that, sure, they're a mite listless, but overall their spirits are good and —

LORRAINE. Oh, you boys are in denial. I went out to that ranch of yours yesterday, and every one of those bony cows was lying around like a welfare mother. And correct me if I'm wrong, but it didn't seem like there was one hundred of them, either.

MAGGIE. Is that right, Bud? Did some of our cows run away?

BUD. No, Mayor Maggie. We got electrified security. What's happened with the twenty-two dead cows is that —

LORRAINE and MAGGIE. Twenty-two dead cows?!

ROY. It's better to think of it as a streamlining of the herd. It's a perfectly common anomaly.

MAGGIE. Bud, it's time for you boys to wake up and smell the music: We obviously got ourselves a predicament here.

BUD. All right! I admit it!

## "ANOTHER DEAD COW"
### (Bud, Ned, Roy, Lorraine, Maggie)

BUD.
  BOSSIE'S THIN AS A FISHIN' POLE.
NED.
  BESSIE'S FLAT AS A FLOUNDER.
ROY.
  LITTLE BONNIE, GOD REST HER SOUL,
  WAS BARELY ONE QUARTER-POUNDER.
BUD.
  I CHECK MY BOVINE MANUAL
  AND I FIND NO DEFINITION;
BUD and NED.
  EVEN THIS REVISED EDITION
  DOES NOT MENTION MALNUTRITION!
ROY.
  GUSSIE DIED OF A HACKIN' COUGH.
  CLARA DROWNED IN THE FEEDING TROUGH.
ALL THREE.
  WHY WOULD THE LORD WANNA CARRY THEM
  OFF?

| ALL but BUD. | BUD. |
|---|---|
| DANG! | DANG! |
| WE GOT ANOTHER | WE GOT ANOTHER |

| | |
|---|---|
| DEAD COW<br>AND THE RENT IS<br>OVERDUE. | DEAD COW … <br><br>WE'RE FACIN' POVERTY! |

ALL but ROY.
  GOT ANOTHER
  DEAD COW
  AND WE'RE UP TO
  TWENTY-TWO.

ROY. *(On phone, covers receiver.)* Better make that twenty-three!

ALL.
  SWEET JESUS, NOW I'M PETRIFIED …

NED.
  THEY'RE GONNA REPOSSESS MY DOUBLE-WIDE!

ALL.
*(Beginning to point fingers.)*
  GOT ANOTHER DEAD COW
  AND I'M THINKING OF BLAMING Y —

MAGGIE.  — You wanna be watching that kind of talk, let's not go there. Everybody, let's pull together on this.

BUD.  I'm telling you, this town is cursed! First the coal mines dried up on us, now all the cows are dropping like flies. I don't know what to do, I wasn't cut out to be a rancher! What I wouldn't give to be a coal miner again. *(All cough. Bud's handkerchief turns black from the contents of his lungs.)*

ROY.  Those were the good old days.

MAGGIE.  All right, let's guide this train of thought back toward the depot. We gotta figure out what's wrong with these cows.

ALL.
  SOMETHING'S MAKING 'EM COUGH AND WHEEZE,
  SLOWLY DRIVING THEM TO THEIR KNEES …

BUD.
  IT'S GOTTA BE SOME *CONTAGIOUS DISEASE!*

ALL.
  A *PLAGUE!*

| ALL but MAGGIE. | MAGGIE. |
|---|---|
| WE GOT ANOTHER<br>DEAD COW<br>AND WE DON'T<br>KNOW WHY | WE GOT ANOTHER<br>DEAD COW<br>AND WE DON'T<br>KNOW WHY |

| | |
|---|---|
| THEY DIE … | THEY DIE … |
| | We got to find |
| | a link! … |
| ALL but BUD. | BUD. |
|    GOT ANOTHER DEAD |    GOT ANOTHER DEAD |
|    COW |    COW |
|    AND APOCALYPSE |    AND APOCALYPSE |
|    DRAWS NIGH. |    DRAWS NIGH. |
| | |
| | You went to |
| | college, think! |

ALL.
   WELL, SOMETHING'S BOUND TO RAISE A FLAG,
LORRAINE.
   Like that little Bat Boy
   they found in the bag? …
*(Long pause. A new, horrible possibility dawns on them.)*
ALL.
   GOT ANOTHER DEAD COW …
   GOT ANOTHER D —
   GOT ANO —
   G —
   … GOT ANOTHER DEAD COW
   BUT I'M TELLIN' YOU NOW
   I AM MAKIN' A VOW
   BY THE SWEAT OF MY BROW
   GONNA FIGGER OUT WHO AND WHAT AND HOW AND *WHY!*
*(Townsfolk begin to disperse, each lost in thought. They address the air, not looking at each other:)*
ROY. It *is* like they've been bled …
NED, MAGGIE, BUD and LORRAINE.
   WHY! …
BUD. Do you think Dr. Parker will put it down?
NED, MAGGIE, ROY and LORRAINE.
   WHY! …
LORRAINE. Well, Dr. Parker's a good man.
NED, MAGGIE, ROY, and BUD.
   WHY! …
LORRAINE. I'm sure he'll kill it!

ALL.
  WHY!!! ...
*(Thunder.)*


## Scene 5


*Parker home. The front door opens. Dr. Thomas Parker enters, carrying two dead geese around his neck. He holds a shotgun in one hand. He wears a hunting knife on his belt. He is drunk. He doesn't see Bat Boy yet.*


PARKER.  Sorry I'm so late! The roads are all mud and the lights are out all over town! But I got a limit! Hello! *(Parker regards his dead geese.)* I'll call this one Fricassee, and this one I'll call Cacciatore. Heh-heh ... I was just getting ready to pack it in when the wind starts kicking up, and this perfect formation of honkers comes banking in from the West, and — *(Bangs into the cage.)* Aah! What's the big cage doing out? Another stray? *(Parker takes a candle and walks over to the cage. The light from the candle illuminates Parker's reaction to Bat Boy. Thunder.)* Sweet wounded Jesus! How did you get here? *(Parker goes to his doctor's bag, pulls out a flask and takes a drink. He takes out a pocket tape recorder and studies Bat Boy, dictating:)*
PARKER.
  MAMMAL, HUMANOID,
  ADOLESCENT MALE,
  MASSIVE OVERBITE,
  FEVERISH AND PALE.
  CLAWED PREHENSILE FEET,
  SORES THAT WILL NOT HEAL,
*(He picks up Meredith's stew pot and considers it.)*
  STARVING, BUT WON'T EAT.
    ... I KNOW HOW YOU FEEL.
*(Parker pauses, then pulls from his doctor's bag a syringe and fills it with a pink liquid from a vial.)* Well, this'll put one of us out of our misery. *(Parker approaches Bat Boy with the syringe. He is just about to pierce Bat Boy's neck with the needle when Meredith enters and ... )*
MEREDITH.  Thomas, no! *(Parker turns to her. The syringe is still poised.)*

PARKER. What?

MEREDITH. Please. Don't.

PARKER. Well, why not? *(He leans in to inject Bat Boy.)*

MEREDITH. Please!

PARKER. *(Annoyed.)* What!?

MEREDITH. Let him live. He's just a boy.

PARKER. You know what this is, don't you?

MEREDITH. Yes, I know. You could save him if you wanted to, couldn't you? You could make him well again?

PARKER. Are you kidding me? The ranchers would go nuts. They're already blaming their problems on anything they can think of.

MEREDITH. But if you wanted to …

PARKER. I can hear it now. "There goes Dr. Parker. He couldn't manage to save our cattle, but he saved the Bat Boy. He's Hope Falls' finest citizen, maybe we won't run him out on a rail after all … "

MEREDITH. … but we could just keep him here in the house …

PARKER. … They'll have my head for something like this, Meredith. And I'll bet you dollars to donuts that Sheriff Reynolds expects me to put it down, don't try to tell me any different. There's just no way around this. Sorry, little fella, there's just no way around it. *(He moves to Bat Boy, pushes his head to the side and bares his neck for the needle.)*

MEREDITH. *(Falling to her knees.)* No, please! I'm begging you. *(Parker pulls up short.)* You can't just kill him like an animal. Please, please.

PARKER. So, now you've got all this love in your heart, do you?

MEREDITH. You have to let him live. We can take care of him.

PARKER. Where'd you find the room for all this love in your heart all of a sudden?

MEREDITH. We have to let him live.

PARKER. Who do you love?

MEREDITH. Oh, please, Thomas.

PARKER. Tell me who you love. Who do you love, Meredith?

MEREDITH. Please don't do this.

PARKER. Me, right? It's me you love.

MEREDITH. Of course I do. I'm your wife.

PARKER. *(Turning back to Bat Boy.)* You haven't been a wife to me in years.

MEREDITH. I could be.

PARKER. *(Freezes.)* Tonight? *(Beat.)* Tonight?

MEREDITH. Let me get you a drink.

PARKER.

*(Grabbing her hand.)*

BUT THERE WAS A TIME, YOU KNOW,
  WHEN YOU WOULD SMILE AT ME …
MEREDITH.  *(To herself; "there he goes again")* Oh no …
PARKER.
  ONCE LONG AGO, THERE WAS LOVE IN YOUR EYES.
  YOU WERE SO LIGHT IN MY ARMS,
  WE DANCED FIVE HOURS OR MORE,
  WE WERE THE LAST ON THE FLOOR,
  WITH THE SUN SOON TO RISE …
  THE BAND PLAYED ONE FINAL SONG,
  AND WE WERE HUMMING ALONG:
*(Parker impulsively grabs Meredith and dances with her. Meredith, with manufac-*
*tured smile, plays along and gently tries to get the syringe away from him. Parker*
*keeps it out of her reach, still dancing.)*
  OH, DANCE WITH ME DARLING,
  WE HAVEN'T DANCED SINCE
  I DON'T KNOW WHEN,
  OH, DANCE WITH ME DARLING,
  WON'T YOU EMBRACE ME,
  KISS ME IN CASE WE
  DON'T MEET AGAIN.
  I'VE HEARD A RUMOR,
  BARELY A WHISPER,
  CLAIMING THAT WE WERE THROUGH.
  SO DANCE WITH ME DARLING,
  SHOW THEM THAT IT'S NOT TRUE.
*(Bat Boy moans, drawing their attention. They stare at him.)*
MEREDITH.  So you'll do it?
PARKER.  So *you'll* do it?
MEREDITH.  Yes.
PARKER.  Tell me you love me, Meredith.
MEREDITH.  I will. *(Moves to exit.)*
PARKER.  Things are really turning around for us, aren't they?
MEREDITH.  That's right, dear. *(Meredith exits.)*
PARKER.  *(To Bat Boy.)* Did you hear that? I guess that makes us pals.
  'CAUSE NOW I CAN'T SAY NO,
  TONIGHT SHE SMILED AT ME:
  JUST GOES TO SHOW,
  SOMEONE UP THERE STILL CARES.

I PRAYED THIS DAY WOULD ARRIVE,
WHEN SHE'D RETURN TO MY ARMS;
NOW IF I KEEP YOU ALIVE,
I CAN JOIN HER UPSTAIRS.
I SEE A WAY TO PROCEED,
SO WE BOTH CAN GET WHAT WE NEED.

*(Parker dances around the room, humming. He puts out candles. Ghostly figures appear. They are the Voices In His Head.)*

PARKER and VOICES IN HIS HEAD.
OH, DANCE WITH ME, DARLING,
LA DA DA DA DA,
DA DA, DA DA,

*(He picks up a basin, collects the geese, approaches Bat Boy.)*

OH, DANCE WITH ME DARLING,
DA DA DA DA DA,
DA DA DA DA DA,
DA DA DA DA.

*(Parker picks up Bat Boy and cradles him in his arms.)*

PARKER.
SURELY IT'S MORE THAN MOONLIGHT AND MUSIC.
SURELY IT'S MORE THAN WINE.
SO DANCE WITH ME DARLING,
SHOW THEM THAT YOU'RE STILL MINE! …

*(Lightning flashes and with each explosion of light we see a tableau: FLASH! Parker cuts the necks of the geese. Darkness. Thunder. FLASH! Blood pours into the basin. Bat Boy rouses slightly. Darkness. Thunder. FLASH! Parker holds Bat Boy's head above the basin. Bat Boy screeches. Darkness. Thunder. FLASH! Parker submerges Bat Boy's head in the basin of blood. Darkness. Thunder. FLASH! Bat Boy, his face covered in blood, screams like a beast. Darkness. Silence. A single spotlight finds Bat Boy's face. He pants heavily. Something lifts him into the air. Lights go wild. Bat Boy howls over fractured and demented music.)*

SCARY CHORUS.
AH AH AH AH AH AH AH …
AAAAAAAHHHH!

*(Lights change back to the Parker home. Bat Boy is exhausted but clearly healthier. Parker sings to Bat Boy, to the absent Meredith, or both.)*

PARKER.                                    VOICES IN HIS HEAD.
SURELY THE GODS MUST
WANT US TOGETHER,

33

DON'T FIGHT THEIR
GRAND DESIGN,
NO, DANCE WITH ME,
DARLING …                    AAH AH AH AH AH!
DANCE WITH ME,
DARLING …                    AAH AH AH AH AH!
*(Parker sweeps the bewildered Bat Boy up in his arms and dances him round.)*
AND BE FOREVER
MINE!                        AAH AH AH AH AH, AHH!!!


## Scene 6


*Hospital room. A doctor, Mrs. Taylor, Rick and Ron stand around Ruthie's hospital bed. Ruthie is in some pain.*


MRS. TAYLOR.
   SLEEP LITTLE RUTHIE BABY, DON'T YOU FEAR NO BAT BOY,
   DREAM ABOUT THE ANGELS FLOATING ROUND YOUR HEAD.
   SLEEP ON A PILLOW MADE FROM FLUFFY CLOUDS AND RAINBOWS,
*(Sheriff enters. Mrs. Taylor turns round to face him.)*
   WHILE MAMA CAN'T BE*LIEVE*
*(Shouting.)*
   *THAT LITTLE FREAK AIN'T DEAD!*
SHERIFF. Now, Mrs. Taylor, I sympathize with your situation …
RUTHIE. *(Very weak voice.)* — The monster. The monster …
MRS. TAYLOR. *(Turning from Sheriff.)* Oh, my baby.
RICK. Take it easy, Ruthie.
RUTHIE. Monster!
RON. Calm down, Ruthie …
MRS. TAYLOR. Listen to your brothers, honey … Sshhh, sshhh. I know. Try to save your strength. *(Mrs. Taylor hugs Ruthie and kisses her on the forehead.)*
DOCTOR. I don't understand why her blood isn't clotting, but other than that she's doing all right. She's going to be fine, Mrs. Taylor.
MRS. TAYLOR. Thank you, doctor. *(The doctor exits.)*
RICK. We want that thing dead, Sheriff!

RON. Yeah!

SHERIFF. Now, boys, I understand.

MRS. TAYLOR. I can't believe Dr. Parker didn't kill it.

RICK. It's in their house!

MRS. TAYLOR. Why, even when my Ricky borrowed that truck from the construction site, you put him in jail for a whole weekend! Why does that bat freak get special attention?

SHERIFF. Dr. Parker did put him in a cage ...

RICK. That cage'll never hold him!

RON. What if he gets out and attacks us again?

MRS. TAYLOR. (Smacking Ron on the head.) Oh no! Don't you say that, Ron. (Grabbing sons into a hug.) Not my babies. I couldn't bear it. I just couldn't bear it if that beast got out and hurt one of my children. (She sobs.)

RICK and RON. It's okay, Mama/Don't worry ...

SHERIFF. Don't worry, Mrs. Taylor. I've seen the boy, and I'll admit he looks peculiar, but he's not exactly what you'd call a —

RUTHIE. Monster! Monster!

MRS. TAYLOR. Hush, baby doll.

RUTHIE. Bat monster ... bat monster ... BAT MONSTER!

MRS. TAYLOR.
> SLEEP LITTLE RUTHIE BABY NO ONE'S GONNA HURT YOU,
> SHERIFF'S GONNA HAVE THAT LITTLE FREAK DESTROYED,
> OR IF HE'S A COWARD AND HE WON'T PROTECT MY CHILDREN,
> MAMA'S GONNA GET THE SHERIFF UNEMPLOYED.

MRS. TAYLOR, RICK and RON.
> SLEEP LITTLE RUTHIE BABY DON'T YOU FEAR NO BAT BOY,
> MAMA'S GONNA HUNT HIM DOWN AND BRING HIM HERE.
> THEN YOU CAN SKIN HIM AND WEAR HIM AS A JACKET,
> AND WE'LL STRING A NECKLACE WITH A DRIED BAT EAR.

## Scene 7

*Parker living room. Bright morning light. Kitchen table center. Meredith sits at the table with Bat Boy, whom she has dressed.*

MEREDITH. Hellooo? Hellooo? Can you say hello? You can do it. Look at my lips. *(She points to her lips.)* Lips. Helllllooooo. Helllllooooo. *(Bat Boy turns away and grunts.)* You don't want to say hello? That's okay. We've got time. *(Bat Boy moves about the room sniffing things and grunting. Meredith watches for a while. Then she gets an idea. Meredith imitates one of Bat Boy's grunts. Bat Boy looks at her. Meredith makes the grunt again. Bat Boy looks at her for a second, then makes the same grunt again. Meredith makes another grunt. Bat Boy responds. Meredith makes a different grunt. Bat Boy imitates it.)* Helllooooo …

BAT BOY. Eeeleeee … *(This goes on, ad-lib: Meredith breaks the word down into syllables and communicates with Bat Boy through a series of more elaborate grunts that approach the sound of the word "hello." Bat Boy gets better and better at it, until … )* Hhhhelllooo.

MEREDITH. That is *very* good. Hello.

BAT BOY. Hello.

MEREDITH. *(She applauds and smiles.)* Good. *(Bat Boy copies her — he applauds and smiles.)* Now, can you say "boy"?

BAT BOY. Boy.

MEREDITH. That is very good.

BAT BOY. Boy!

MEREDITH. Yes, you are. You're a boy.

BAT BOY. Boy. Boy. Boy, boy, boy, boy, boy, boy, boy, boy, boy, boy!

MEREDITH. And you're a smart boy, too. We'll turn you into a proper young man in no time. *(Meredith opens a children's book and … )*

## "SHOW YOU A THING OR TWO"
### *(Bat Boy, Meredith, Shelley, Parker)*

| MEREDITH. | BAT BOY. |
|---|---|
| HERE IS A CAT. | HEE BA MA CAT. |
| THERE IS A GOOSE. | ZA BA ZA GOOSE. |
| THIS IS A RAT. | ZI BI ZA WAT. |
| AND THAT IS A MOOSE. | BA BA BA BA BOOSE. |
| THE CAT CREPT UP BEHIND | |
| THE GOOSE | |
| BUT THEN AWAY IT FLEW. | FLÜ. |
| THE RAT WAS JEALOUS | |
| OF A MOOSE | |
| WHO LOVED A KANGAROO. | RÜ. |
| THE CAT AND RAT MADE UP | |
| AND FOUND | |
| A FLAT IN TIMBUKTU. | TÜ. |
| AND NOW, | AND NOW, |
| REVIEW. | REVIEW … |
| WE READ THE WHOLE | |
| WAY THROUGH! | |
| | CAA, GOOSH, |
| | RAA, MOOSH. |
| | KAGAROOW, |
| | TIBUKTOOW. |
| UNDERSTAND? | YESH I DO! |
| GOOD FOR YOU! | |
| I'LL SHOW YOU A | |
| THING OR TWO, | TWO, |
| I'LL TEACH YOU TO | |
| NAME IT, | NANE IT, |
| SURE IT'S TOUGH BUT | |
| YOU'LL TAME IT, | TANE IT, |
| AND ONCE YOU'VE BEAT IT … | GGRGRWBRRGH! … |
| *(Bat Boy tries to eat the book.)* | |
| OH, WAIT! DON'T EAT IT … | OH … |

I'LL SHOW YOU THE WAY IT'S
DONE,
THEN I'LL LEAVE IT TO YOU,
AND WHADDAYA KNOW, YOU MAY
SHOW ME A THING OR TWO!

*(Meredith takes the children's book from Bat Boy and crosses the stage. Shelley enters, in her school uniform.)*

SHELLEY.  Hi, Mom!

MEREDITH.  Hello, Shelley. How was school?

SHELLEY.  It was great! How's Bat Boy doing today?

MEREDITH.  *Edgar's* coming along nicely. Today we're learning etiquette. Why don't you introduce yourself, Shelley?

| SHELLEY. | BAT BOY. |
|---|---|
| HOW DO YOU DO? | HOW DO YOU DO? |
| LOVELY, AND YOU? | LOVELY, AND YOU? |
| WON'T YOU SIT DOWN? | WON'T YOU SIT DOWN? |
| DON'T MIND IF I DO. | DON'T MIND IF I DO. |
| THE WEATHER WOULD | |
| BE PERFECT | |
| IF IT WEREN'T QUITE | |
| SO HOT. | HOT. |

| MEREDITH. | |
|---|---|
| I WISH WE HAD MORE | |
| SANDWICHES, | |
| THAT BUTLER SHOULD | |
| BE SHOT. | SHOT. |

| MEREDITH and SHELLEY. | |
|---|---|
| BUT WON'T YOU STAY | |
| THE NIGHT, | |
| WE'RE HAVING | |
| DINNER ON THE | |
| YACHT! | YACHT? |

| MEREDITH. | |
|---|---|
| NOW READY — | WHAT? |
| OR NOT, | NOT! |
| SHOW ME WHAT | |
| YOU'VE GOT! | |
| | BOW DEEP, |
| | KISS HAND, |

PULL CHAIR,
LOOK BLAND,
POUR THE TEA,
PASS THE JAM.

ARE WE CLEAR? YES MA'AM!

*(Bat Boy spills the tea and dishes go flying. Bat Boy panics. Meredith calms him.)*

MEREDITH. BAT BOY.

I'LL SHOW YOU A THING
OR TWO, *[Sniff]*
DON'T CRY, IT'S OKAY, DEAR; *[Sniff, Sniff]*
ROME'S NOT BUILT IN A DAY,
DEAR. HAH?
A BIT MORE SCHOOLING;

*(Wiping his drool off her shoulder.)*

A LOT LESS DROOLING.

MEREDITH and SHELLEY.

EASY DOES IT, THAT'S HOW
IT'S DONE,
SOON YOU'LL PICK UP YOUR
CUE,
THEN WHADDAYA KNOW,
YOU MAY
SHOW US A THING OR TWO!

*(Parker enters with a doctor's bag.)*

PARKER. Honey, I'm home!

SHELLEY. Hi, Daddy! How was work?

PARKER. Great! How is Edgar coming along?

MEREDITH. This week's been a little rocky.

SHELLEY. We're trying flash cards!

*(They produce flash cards with pictures. Bat Boy guesses:)*

BAT BOY. MEREDITH. SHELLEY. PARKER.

CHAMPS ELYSÉES?
PARTHENON.
GREAT WHITE WAY?
EVERGLADES.
BERLIN WALL?
AUTOBAHN.
CARNEGIE HALL?
ICE CAPADES.

PENTAGON?

                                        GOLDEN GATE.

AMAZON?

                                                    RIO GRANDE.

TAJ MAJAL!

                                        EMPIRE STATE.

WAILING WALL?

                        DISNEYLAND.

*(Bat Boy weeps in defeat. Parker takes him aside.)*

PARKER.  Perhaps I should have a word with the boy. Let me talk to him over here for a moment!

    I'LL SHOW YOU A THING OR TWO,

    SURE, KID, YOU FEEL WEARY,

    HEAD'S ALL FUZZY AND BLEARY,

    I KNOW YOU'RE LEERY,

    BUT HERE'S MY THEORY:

*(Parker pulls a rat from his bag and breaks its neck. Bat Boy feeds on its head, taking several strong swallows of blood.)*

    KEEP SLUGGIN', THAT'S HOW IT'S DONE,

    SOON YOU'RE BOUND TO BREAK THROUGH!

    AND WHADDAYA KNOW, YOU MAY —

BAT BOY.

    Wait a minute!

PARKER and MEREDITH.

    WHADDAYA KNOW, YOU MAY —

BAT BOY.

    I think I've got it!

PARKER, MEREDITH and SHELLEY.

    WHADDAYA KNOW, YOU MAY —

BAT BOY.

    Eureka!

PARKER, MEREDITH and SHELLEY.

    Show me!

*(Bat Boy, evolving at a lightning pace, rapidly identifies flash cards, photographs, videotapes, records:)*

BAT BOY.

    BROOKLYN BRIDGE,

    LENIN'S TOMB,

    WATERGATE,

RAINBOW ROOM!
RUBY RIDGE, LIBERTY BELL!
BERING STRAIT, BATES MOTEL!
*SPARTACUS, FARGO* AND *ANCHORS AWEIGH,*
*LOVE STORY, KEY LARGO, REMAINS OF THE DAY*!
PUCCINI, COLE PORTER, ROSSINI, *OTELLO,*
BELLINI, WAYNE SHORTER AND ELVIS COSTELLO!

*(Dance break with whooping.)*

SHELLEY.  Mom, Edgar just finished his essay for his high-school equivalency exam!

BAT BOY.

*(Produces a blue examination booklet and reads.)*

I WILL DISCUSS COPERNICUS, WHO RUINED ALL OUR FUN,
AND SHOWED WE'RE JUST A BALL OF DUST THAT LIMPS AROUND THE SUN.
WHICH BRINGS ME THEN TO DARWIN, WHEN HE BENT US OUT OF SHAPE
AS HE BEGAN TO PROVE THAT MAN IS NEPHEW TO AN APE.
WE WERE ANNOYED WHEN DOCTOR FREUD DECLARED IT'S NOT A SOUL,
IT IS YOUR BLIND SUBCONSCIOUS MIND THAT'S ALWAYS IN CONTROL.
BUT I SUBMIT THAT ANY TWIT, IF HE HAS EYES TO SEE,
CAN SEIZE HIS FATE; SELF-EDUCATE; AND TURN OUT JUST LIKE ME!

*(Parkers cheer. Bat Boy runs offstage. A chorus appears.)*

ALL.

SHIRT, SHOES, PANTS, VEST.
CAN'T GO OUT THERE UNDERDRESSED.
COLLAR PRESSED, LOOK YOUR BEST,
AND WON'T THEY BE IMPRESSED!, CAUSE:

*(Bat Boy reenters wearing cap and gown.)*

| BAT BOY. | PARKERS and CHORUS. |
|---|---|
| I'LL SHOW 'EM | YOU'LL SHOW 'EM |
| A THING OR TWO, | A THING OR TWO, |
| | |
| I WAS DIRTY AND ROWDY, | ROWDY! |
| EVEN DRESSED A BIT | |
| DOWDY, | DOWDY! |

BUT NOW SAY:
TO A SUMMA CUM LAUDE!
I'LL SHOW 'EM THE
WAY IT'S DONE,
BUT NO APPLAUSE,
I'M NOT THROUGH!
I'M GONNA VINCE VAN
GOGH 'EM,
AND PLATO,
AND EDGAR ALLAN POE 'EM,

AND JACQUES COUSTEAU
'EM,
HOUDINI,
GONNA JACKIE O 'EM,
BOTTICELLI,
LARRY, CURLY AND MOE
'EM!
AND WHADDAYA KNOW,
ONCE YOU —
YOU SUDDENLY GROW TO
BE —
SO BUDDY, I'M GOING TO
SHOW 'EM ALL A THING …
OR …
TWO!

OR TWO!

OR TWO!

"HOWDY"!
SUMMA CUM LAUDE!
YOU'LL SHOW 'EM THE
WAY IT'S DONE,
BUT NO APPLAUSE,
HE'S NOT THROUGH!

AND HENRY THOREAU 'EM,
AND CATO,

GONNA JEAN COCTEAU 'EM,

FELLINI,
AND MICHELANGELO 'EM,
MARILYN MONROE 'EM,
MACHIAVELLI,

LEARN TO CRAWL, AH! …

TEN FEET TALL, AH! …

SHOW 'EM ALL A THING …
OR …
YOU'LL SHOW 'EM A
THING OR TWO!
YOU'LL SHOW 'EM A
THING OR TWO!
YOU'LL SHOW 'EM A
THING OR TWO!

ALL.
*SHOW 'EM A THING OR TWO!*

# Scene 8

*Hope Falls Town Hall. Sheriff, Maggie, Bud, Jackie, Lorraine, Roy, Parker.*

CROWD. *(Ad-lib hubbub.)* It'll be a disaster. / What's the speaking order? / I think I speak first.

MAGGIE. Settle down! I hereby call this special meeting of the Town Council to order. Item One. Let's discuss safety issues as they relate to this weekend's Revival Meeting. Sheriff?

SHERIFF. Okey-doke. Dr. Parker, thank you for coming here tonight. Let me get right to the point. There's a sense of unease … afoot. No one's saying anything against you, but, well … It's important for the moment … for the revival. We thought maybe you could just take the boy out of town for the weekend.

PARKER. I can assure all of you as a veterinarian that the boy is not a danger. Edgar is not the same wild creature you brought to my home, Sheriff. Meredith has done wonders with him. Why, he's practically a member of the family.

BUD. Oh, for Pete's sake, we got Ruthie Taylor still in the hospital, she's just not getting any better, and I've got a sinking suspicion that your Bat Boy is responsible for the cattle plague!

SHERIFF. — Now, Bud, there's no evidence that links —

BUD. Sheriff — if you don't start whistling the right tune, I've got half a mind to run against you come election day. *(Big hubbub.)*

SHERIFF. Pipe down, people! *(Pulling Dr. Parker aside.)* Dr. Parker …

## "CHRISTIAN CHARITY REPRISE"
### (Sheriff, Parker, Ned, Bud, Lorraine, Townsperson #2, Maggie)

SHERIFF.
*(Aside to Parker.)*
  IT'S NOT ABOUT THESE DUMB ELECTIONS.
PARKER.
  Never said it was.

SHERIFF.
　DON'T WANT THE CART BEFORE THE HORSE.
PARKER.
　Of course, nobody does.
SHERIFF.
*(Louder for everyone's benefit.)*
　BUT SOME OF MY CONSTIT'CHENS
　CLAIM HE'S SKULKIN' THROUGH THEIR KITCHENS,
　AND SOON I MAY HAVE NO RECOURSE
　BUT TO ENFORCE THE LAW! —
BUD.
　With deadly force!
*(Hubbub.)*

| LORRAINE. | BUD. |
|---|---|
| SO THERE IT IS, DOC, | |
| SPELLED OUT PLAIN, | |
| | So are we |
| | clear? |
| MAGGIE. | |
| YOU WILL TAKE NO ACTION | |
| THAT COULD DERAIL THIS | |
| TRAIN. | You hear? |
| MAGGIE, ROY, LORRAINE, NED and SHERIFF. | |
| YOU SHOULD JUST BE GRATEFUL | |
| WE DON'T HANG HIM FROM A TREE, | — YEAH! |
| BUT DON'T YOU GO TESTIN' OUR | DON'T YOU GO |
| | TESTIN' OUR |
| CHRISTIAN | CHRISTIAN |
| CHARITY! | CHARITY! |
| SO SHIP HIM | SO SHIP HIM |
| OUT, DOC, | OUT, DOC, |
| DON'T CARE | DON'T CARE |
| WHERE, | WHERE, |
| | We think |
| | that's fair! |
| TAKE THE LONG WAY HOME | |
| BECAUSE — | |

| | |
|---|---|
| ROY. | BUD. |
| He's foulin' the air! | |
| | I swear! |
| MAGGIE, ROY, LORRAINE, | |
| NED and SHERIFF. | |
| DOC, WE NEED | DOC, WE NEED |
| A QUARANTINE, | A QUARANTINE, |
| WE WANT A | WE WANT A |
| GUARANTEE. | GUARANTEE … |
| HE CAN'T BE ALLOWED TO COME. | |
| | He'll cause |
| | *pandemonium!* |
| SO SHAPE UP | SO SHAPE UP |
| AND SHOW | AND SHOW |
| US SOME | US SOME |
| CHRISTIAN — | CHRISTIAN — |

PARKER. — This is going to be hard on Meredith. But I give you my word. Edgar will not attend the revival.

BUD. Your word of honor?

PARKER. My word of honor.

BUD. Well. All right. *(Bud dramatically extends his hand. Parker shakes it.)*

SHERIFF. Oh, now that's just great. I knew you'd be reasonable about this. *(Everyone ad-libs "thank-yous" and shakes Dr. Parker's hand as he exits.)*

CROWD. Thank you, Dr. Parker. / Glad we worked it out. / You're a good man, Dr. Parker.

ALL but PARKER.

THANK GOD YOU'LL BE SHOWIN' SOME CHRISTIAN CHARITY. *(Through gritted teeth.)*

AND SOME DANG SENSE.

# Scene 9

*Parker home — living room. Bat Boy is standing downstage wearing linen pants and a light cotton shirt. Shelley puts a linen sport coat on him. She turns him around and looks at him.*

SHELLEY. You look great.

BAT BOY. *(Very proper English accent.)* Thank you, Shelley, you're looking splendid yourself.

SHELLEY. You look, like, you're ready to go to the dance hall in Wheeling.

BAT BOY. Oh. *(A bow.)* May I have the pleasure, Miss Shelley?

SHELLEY. *(A curtsy.)* Why, I'd be delighted, Master Edgar. *(Bat Boy puts both hands on Shelley's waist. A moment as they take each other in. Shelley recovers first.)* Um ... no. It's like this. Your right hand stays there, but your left goes up here.

BAT BOY. Oh, yes, I see. *(Another moment as they stare into each other's eyes. They awkwardly start to dance ... In the kitchen Meredith readies a tea service.)*

PARKER. It's just for the weekend.

MEREDITH. I don't like the Town Council telling me what to do with my family.

PARKER. I know. I don't either. But these are stubborn people, and we're not holding many cards, dear. I think we have to let them win this one.

MEREDITH. Well, I suppose it will be good for Edgar to get away for a few days.

PARKER. Thank you, Meredith. *(Meredith and Parker enter the living room.)*

MEREDITH. Edgar! Shelley! *(Bat Boy and Shelley separate. Meredith brings a tea service out on a tray and sets it at the head of the table. Parker follows.)* Oh! You're already here. Don't you look lovely, Edgar.

BAT BOY. Thank you, Mrs. Parker. You're looking splendid yourself.

MEREDITH. Why, thank you. Those BBC language tapes are really helping your diction.

SHELLEY. And his vocabulary.

BAT BOY. Indubitably. *(All laugh.)*

MEREDITH. Come, let's sit down. *(Parker sits at the head of the table, and prepares to pour tea.)*

BAT BOY. May I serve?

MEREDITH.  Of course you may. *(Parker slides the tea service to Bat Boy as Shelley and Meredith take their places at the table. Bat Boy flawlessly serves tea and sandwiches during the following.)*

BAT BOY.  You know, I was reading the newspaper this morning.

MEREDITH.  Is that right?

BAT BOY.  Yes. And I noticed that, beginning tomorrow, the Reverend Billy Hightower is holding a weekend revival. And, as I have just finished reading the Bible again, it would mean so much to me if I could attend.

SHELLEY.  Yes! That would be so cool. You could wear your new suit and I could wear my new dress. Oh my God. I can just see everybody's faces.

BAT BOY.  I did think it would be a nice coming out for me.

PARKER.  Actually, we were thinking that maybe we'd go away on a camping trip for the weekend. Just us? Alone in the woods?

MEREDITH.  Wouldn't that be nice, Edgar?

BAT BOY.  Oh, yes! But we can do that anytime. The revival is the social event of the season.

MEREDITH.  Oh, Edgar, I feel horrible telling you no, but it just isn't the right time for that sort of thing.

SHELLEY.  But the way people talk about him, it's not fair.

PARKER.  *Shelley.* This is not up for discussion right now.

BAT BOY.  *(To Shelley.)* What is it that people … say about me?

PARKER.  People can be very cruel. It doesn't mean anything about y —

BAT BOY.  — They say *cruel* things? Is that it?

MEREDITH.  Some people —

BAT BOY.  — they don't know me.

PARKER.  That's why they're so cruel.


## "A HOME FOR YOU REPRISE"
### *(Bat Boy)*


BAT BOY.
　BUT I'M NOT HERE TO HARM THEM,
　I ONLY WANT TO LEARN,
　THEY ALL WALK IN SUNLIGHT,
　I DESERVE A TURN.
　I WANT TO KNOW MY NEIGHBORS,
　I'M NOT SOME GARDEN GNOME …

WHY CAN'T I MAKE THIS WORLD MY HOME?

MEREDITH. Edgar, this cannot happen. Not just now. Let's just ... can't we just have a nice trip to the woods?

SHELLEY. And when can it happen, Mother? Next week?

MEREDITH. I don't know.

SHELLEY. Next month?

MEREDITH. Perhaps.

SHELLEY. Next year for sure though, right?

MEREDITH. I can't say.

SHELLEY. Maybe never?

PARKER. Shelley ...

SHELLEY. May I be excused?

MEREDITH. But you haven't finished your tea, dear.

SHELLEY. May I be excused?

MEREDITH. (Sighs.) Yes, you're excused. (Shelley stomps off.) Edgar, I'm so sorry —

BAT BOY. They're saying horrible things about me!

MEREDITH. Oh, Edgar.

BAT BOY. (Getting agitated.) It's torture to sit here idly while I'm being slandered in public. I can only imagine what they're saying.

PARKER. Edgar, we're not saying you can't go out sometime, just not right —
(Bat Boy cuts Parker off with a wave of his hand.)

BAT BOY.

(To Meredith.)

SOMETHING WAS TROUBLING ME RECENTLY,
WATCHING THE WORLD FROM THIS TABLE,
READING AND DREAMING AND GEN'RALLY GROWING MOLD ...
BUT TODAY I LOOKED UP JUST IN TIME TO SEE
THIS MEDICAL PROGRAM ON CABLE;
ASTONISHED, I RAN TO THE MIRROR AND THERE, BEHOLD!
LOOK HERE, I'VE GOT A NAVEL!

(Bat Boy displays his navel. Meredith and Parker are confused.)

... IT MEANS I'M SOMEONE'S CHILD.
THE DOCTOR MUST HAVE TIED IT WHILE MY MOTHER SMILED ...
WHICH MEANS I MAY BE HUMAN,
COMPLETE WITH FAM'LY TREE.
AND IF YOU'D LET ME GO AND SEE,
THIS WORLD MAY BE A HOME FOR ...

PARKER. Edgar! You have made your request and the answer has been given to you, and that answer is no. That's all.

BAT BOY. *(Rising furiously.)* I might as well be in a cage! You must allow me to show myself!

MEREDITH. *(Softening.)* Oh, Edgar.

PARKER. *(Rising also.)* No!

BAT BOY. Why not?

MEREDITH. Edgar, calm yourself, dear.

BAT BOY. Why not! *(His voice changes to a squeal.)* Why not? Why not?! WHY NOT! *(Bat Boy loses control of himself and breaks down and cries.)*

MEREDITH. Oh, I can't bear it. Thomas, can't we just let him go? Once they meet him for themselves, they'll change their minds, don't you think?

PARKER. *(Stunned.)* Well, no …

MEREDITH. Sure they will. He's so charming, and well-spoken. Once they see what a proper young man he is —

PARKER. No no no no no! Meredith, I'm afraid I have to put my foot down on this. I've given my word of honor.

MEREDITH. Well, surely that's not more important than …

PARKER. My word of honor, Meredith. This would humiliate me.

MEREDITH. But can't you see what this means to him?

BAT BOY. … Please, Dr. Parker …

PARKER. I'm putting my foot down. None of us will attend the revival, and that's final.

MEREDITH. *(Pause.)* Fine, don't go. Shelley and I will go with Edgar.

PARKER. *(Approaching her.)* No, I'm putting my foot down.

MEREDITH. Edgar, I'm afraid we'll have to go without Dr. Parker, but Shelley and I will be there for you.

BAT BOY. Really?

PARKER. But I'm putting my foot down.

MEREDITH. Yes, dear. And the rest of us are going to the revival. It's settled.

BAT BOY. You're not too ashamed of me?

MEREDITH. No, no, Edgar, never.

PARKER. Meredith …

BAT BOY. Oh, this is wonderful.

MEREDITH. *(Ignoring Parker; to Bat Boy, kissing him.)* We're not ashamed of you, Edgar. We love you. We all love you so much. Don't you know that? You do know I love you, don't you? Say that you do.

PARKER. Meredith …

BAT BOY. I know. I love you, too, Mrs. Parker.

PARKER. You made a promise to me.

MEREDITH. *(Kissing him again.)* Oh, Edgar.

49

PARKER. *(Grabbing her.)* How can you do this to me! *(Bat Boy suddenly attacks Parker. Like an animal, Bat Boy pounces on Parker and knocks him to the ground. Bat Boy pins Parker on the ground and is about to bite him on the neck. He is poised in this position when Meredith speaks, stopping the imminent fatal bite.)*

MEREDITH. No! Edgar, dear. Edgar? Honey, let's calm down, okay?

BAT BOY. *(Still over Dr. Parker.)* I, I'm sorry, I —

MEREDITH. I know. Get off Dr. Parker, honey. Come here. Come to me. *(Bat Boy finally dismounts Parker and turns to Meredith.)*

BAT BOY. I'm sorry. I'm so sorry.

MEREDITH. It's all right, come here. *(Embracing him.)* I know, dear. It's just because you're hungry. It's okay now.

BAT BOY. I don't know what happened to me.

MEREDITH. *(To Bat Boy.)* Are you all right?

PARKER. *(Getting up.)* Yes, I'm fine, it's just a — *(Sees Meredith is not paying attention to him.)* Oh.

MEREDITH. *(To Bat Boy.)* It's okay. Edgar, I love you so much.

PARKER.
*(Quietly.)*
    AND SO AT LAST I KNOW,
    YOU WENT AND LIED TO ME …

MEREDITH. *(To Bat Boy.)* We'll get you some food and you'll be okay.

PARKER.
    I SAY BRAVO;
    I WAS FOOLED QUITE A WHILE.

MEREDITH. *(To Parker.)* I think it's time for Edgar's medication.

PARKER.
*(With growing rage.)*
    THOUGH YOU CAME BACK TO MY ARMS,

MEREDITH. *(To Bat Boy.)* Everything will be all right, sweetheart.

PARKER.
    YOU'VE ALWAYS LOVED *HIM* MUCH MORE;

MEREDITH. *(She kisses him; standing up.)* So, tomorrow we'll go to the revival.

PARKER.
    AND EV'RY VOW THAT YOU SWORE
    WAS AS *FALSE* AS YOUR *SMILE!* …

MEREDITH. Edgar, I just know that when everyone sees you for who you really are, it's all going to be be okay. Don't you think so, Thomas?

PARKER. *(Smiling.)* Yes. Yes, I do. Sure, it'll work out. Why, it's gonna be great!

BAT BOY. Really?

MEREDITH. Really?

PARKER. Of course! We'll show them what Edgar's made of. They'll all see it. It'll be fine!

MEREDITH. Right, exactly!

BAT BOY. This is so lovely.

PARKER. I have to do a little work at the lab in the morning, but I'll meet you there. And if anybody has a problem with Edgar, by God, they're going to have to answer to Dr. Parker!

MEREDITH. Did you hear that, Edgar?

PARKER. Meredith, why don't you run up and tell Shelley the good news, and I'll give Edgar his medication?

MEREDITH. All right. Well, this is wonderful! Thank you, Thomas.

PARKER. *(Approaching her.)* Things are really turning around for us, aren't they?

MEREDITH. *(Turning to Bat Boy; kisses him.)* I love you, Edgar. This is all going to be fine, you'll see.

BAT BOY. Thank you, Mrs. Parker. *(Exit Meredith. Parker stares after her. Pause.)* I'm sorry I hurt you.

PARKER. *(Beat.)* Are you hungry, Edgar? *(Bat Boy sobs.)* You're crying. Why are you crying?

BAT BOY. Because I'm hungry.

PARKER. You know that I'll feed you.

BAT BOY. I know. Dr. Parker, in Genesis 9, verse 4, God says to Noah, *"Blood shall ye not eat."*

PARKER. Hmm. Well, that's pretty clear, isn't it?

BAT BOY. A commandment from God Himself! Do you think I'll ever be able to stop?

PARKER. Do you think you can?

BAT BOY. Yes. Maybe.

PARKER. Well, if you think you can, perhaps you can. It's all a matter of will power, I suppose. *(Sets down doctor's bag.)* But, then again, if it's part of your nature, that's a tougher problem for you. *(Parker opens the doctor's bag, revealing a live rabbit.)*

BAT BOY. *(Horrified.)* It's not dead.

PARKER. Hmm?

BAT BOY. It's not dead.

PARKER. Oh. Yes. Well, you don't need me to kill it for you, do you? Hey, perhaps this would be a good time to test yourself. Can you resist? *(Bat Boy whines.)* Try Psalm 23.

BAT BOY. Oh, yes. I see. "Yea, though I walk through the valley of the shadow of Death, I will fear no evil. For Thou art with me. Thy rod and thy staff they comfort me. Thou preparest a table before me in the presence of mine enemies."

*(Parker pulls a syringe from his doctor's bag and he stands behind Bat Boy. The Voices In Parker's Head appear and gather behind Parker.)*


## "COMFORT AND JOY"
### *(Parker, Voices, Meredith, Shelley, Town, Bat Boy)*


| PARKER. | VOICES IN HIS HEAD. |
|---|---|
| YOU LITTLE CREEP, YOU'RE GONNA PAY. | |
| I WON'T BE SHOVED OUT OF THE WAY. | |
| OH NO ... | OH NO! |
| OH NO ... | OH NO. |
| AND I COULD MAKE A SOLID CASE | |
| FOR SMASHING IN YOUR FILTHY FACE. | KILL HIM! |
| *(To Voices:)* | |
| SHUT UP ... | KILL HIM! |
| SHUT UP! ... | |
| I'VE GOT A SPADE AND A BURLAP SACK! | KILL HIM NOW! |
| AND THERE'S A HOLE | |
| IN THE YARD OUT BACK. | KILL HIM NOW! |
| BUT IF I FILL IT SHE'LL ASK ME "WHY," | |
| | KILL HIM NOW! |
| SO I'VE GOT ONE THING TO DO | |
| BEFORE YOU DIE ... | NOW ... NOW ... |
| *(To Voices.)* | |
| WAIT! | |
| *(To Bat Boy.)* | |
| SHE WILL SEE WHAT YOU ARE. | |
| I WILL WIN BACK MY BRIDE. | MY BRIDE. |
| SHE *HERSELF* WILL DECIDE | |
| TO GET RID OF THE BOY. | RID OF THE BOY. |
| SHE'LL ADMIT SHE WAS WRONG, | WAS WRONG, |
| SHE'LL RETURN BEFORE LONG, | 'FORE LONG, |
| SHE'LL BE SINGING A SONG | A SONG ... |
| FULL OF COMFORT AND JOY. | |
| | COMFORT AND JOY. COMFORT AND JOY! |

COMFORT AND JOY!

COMFORT AND
JOY! COMFORT
AND JOY! COM-
FORT AND JOY!
KILL THE BAT BOY,
KILL THE BAT BOY!

*(Lights down on Parker and Bat Boy. Lights up on Shelley and Meredith. Meredith is ironing Shelley's Sunday dress. Shelley is looking on suspiciously.)*

MEREDITH.                                          SHELLEY.

OH, HONEY, I APOLOGIZE:
YOU'VE REALLY OPENED UP MY EYES.      NO WAY.
YES WAY!                                        NO WAY!
YES WAY!
I'M LAYING OUT YOUR SUNDAY BEST,
NOW BRUSH YOUR TEETH AND GET
SOME REST,
ALL RIGHT?                                      NO WAY!
ALL RIGHT!                                      ALL RIGHT!
NOW WHEN THEY SEE HIM
THEY'LL MAKE A FUSS.                       Is that true?
WE GOTTA SMILE LIKE WE
JUST DON'T CARE.                            That's not fair!
THEY PUT THEIR PANTS ON
THE SAME AS US.                              Yes they do …
SO JUST IMAGINE THEM
IN THEIR UNDERWEAR …                     AND THEN THIS
                                                TIME I SWEAR …
HE WILL SHOW THAT HE'S NOT           HE'S NOT —
WHAT THEY'RE TERRIFIED OF.            'FIED OF —
HE WILL SHOW THEM A LOVE              A LOVE —
THEY CAN NEVER DESTROY.               NEVER DESTROY.

MEREDITH and SHELLEY.                   PARKER and VOICES.

IF WE PROVE THAT THEY'RE WRONG,
THEY'LL COME 'ROUND BEFORE LONG,
AND WE'LL ALL SING A SONG
FULL OF COMFORT AND JOY.

                                                COMFORT AND
                                                JOY! YEAH!

53

COMFORT AND JOY!
COMFORT                                   COMFORT
AND JOY!                                  AND …
                                          COMFORT
                                          AND JOY!
                                          COMFORT
                                          AND JOY!
                                          COMFORT
                                          AND JOY!
                                          COMFORT
                                          AND JOY!

PARKER.
 STOP THE BAT BOY!
*(Lights on Sheriff and Townspeople, arguing.)*
SHERIFF. Settle down, people! We want to make sure the Revival goes off with-
out a hitch, so let's go over the schedule. Listen up:
 FROM NINE TO TWELVE HE DOES THE HEALING:
NED. Sheriff …
MAGGIE. You hush up.
SHERIFF.
 AT NOON HE'LL BLESS THE FIELDS AND PLOWS,
ROY. Tractors too?
MAGGIE. Hush up!
SHERIFF.
 THEN LUNCH IS AT ONE-THIRTY …
NED. Sheriff, what about my Gertie!
MAGGIE. Hush!
SHERIFF.
 AND AS IT SEEMS THAT TIME ALLOWS,
 THREE TO TEN: THE BLESSING OF THE COWS!
ALL.
 YES! THE BLESSING OF THE COWS!
 BOY, THAT PREACHER'S A PRO!
 GIVES A HECKUVA SHOW!
LORRAINE. Just like Siegfried and Roy!
ALL.
 HE'LL BRING COMFORT AND JOY!
 SO IF NOTHING GOES WRONG,
 YES, IF NOTHING GOES WRONG,

LORD, IF NOTHING GOES WRONG,
WE'LL HAVE COMFORT AND JOY!
COMFORT AND JOY! COMFORT AND JOY!
LORD, WE NEED SOME COMFORT AND JOY!
ANY MEANS YOU'D CARE TO EMPLOY,
WON'T YOU SEND US COMFORT AND JOY!

*(Lights on Bat Boy, kneeling on the table with the rabbit before him. He clumsily puts his hands together, trying to pray.)*

BAT BOY.

Dear God:
I'M STILL NOT SURE HOW PEOPLE PRAY.
OR WHAT ONE DOES WITH ONE'S HANDS.
BUT PLEASE, MY THIRST GROWS EVERY
DAY.
I FEEL IT BURN IN MY GLANDS.
PLEASE WON'T YOU CHANGE THE WAY
I AM,
OR PROVE I'M HUMAN UNDERNEATH;

| | ENSEMBLE. |
|---|---|
| | OO … |
| OR IF YOU JUST DON'T GIVE A DAMN, | OO … |

*(Bat Boy grabs his incisors, exposing his scary fangs.)*

| | |
|---|---|
| YOU COULD AT *LEATHT* GET RID | |
| OF *THEETHE?* | AAHH!.. |
| IF I CAN'T PROVE THEM WRONG, | AH!.. |
| SHOW ME WHERE I BELONG, | AH! … |
| FOR A HUNGER SO STRONG | AH! … |
| KILLS ALL COMFORT AND | COMFORT AND |
| JOY. | JOY! |
| IF YOU'D MAKE ME COMPLETE. | |
| I'LL AVOID ALL RED MEAT, | |
| I'LL EAT NOTHING BUT SOY | |
| TO HAVE COMFORT | COMFORT |
| AND … | AND … |

*(Parker appears in his coat, carrying his doctor's bag.)*

| PARKER. | BAT BOY, TOWNS-FOLK and SHERIFF. |
|---|---|
| | … JOY … |
| BY NEXT WEEK YOU'LL BE GONE, | … JOY … |
| SIX FEET UNDER MY LAWN. | |
| I'LL HAVE NOBODY TOY | |

55

| | |
|---|---|
| WITH MY COMFORT AND … | COMFORT<br>AND … |
| *(Meredith tucks Shelley in.)*<br>MEREDITH and SHELLEY. | BAT BOY, TOWNS-<br>FOLK, SHERIFF<br>and PARKER. |
| | … JOY … |
| HE WILL COME OUT A CHAMP.<br>IT'S JUST LIKE SUMMER CAMP.<br>THEY'LL GET USED TO THE BOY,<br>HE'LL BRING COMFORT AND … | COMFORT<br>AND … |
| *(Townsfolk cling to each other and pray.)*<br>TOWNSFOLK. | BAT BOY,<br>SHERIFF, PARKER,<br>MEREDITH<br>and SHELLEY. |
| GOD, PLEASE GIVE US YOUR WORD.<br>CURE THE PLAGUE ON THE HERD.<br>WE DON'T MEAN TO ANNOY,<br>BUT SEND COMFORT AND … | … JOY …<br><br><br>COMFORT AND |
| *(Bat Boy is triumphing over hunger. He embraces the rabbit.)*<br>BAT BOY. | ENSEMBLE. |
|   JOY, COMFORT AND JOY,<br>  COMFORT AND JOY!<br>  JOY! |   JOY, JOY, JOY!<br>  COMFORT AND<br>  JOY, JOY …<br>  COMFORT<br>  AND JOY!<br>  COMFORT<br>  AND JOY!<br>  COMFORT AND<br>  JOY! COMFORT<br>  AND … |

*(Parker approaches Bat Boy. With his knife he slashes the rabbit's neck. Blood. Bat Boy watches in horrified slow motion. Parker walks across the stage to Ruthie's hospital room, where she is in bed.)*

RUTHIE. Dr. Parker, what are you doing here?

PARKER. *(With syringe.)* It's not me, Ruthie. The Bat Boy is doing this to you. He's a beast. He's a monster. He can't control himself. We're all going to miss you very much. *(Parker injects Ruthie.)*

RUTHIE. *(Scared.)* Dr. Parker, what are you doing?

PARKER. Don't worry. The Bat Boy will be punished for doing this to you, Ruthie. I'll see to that. *(She convulses.)*

CHORUS.
COMFORT AND JOY, COMFORT AND JOY,
COMFORT AND JOY, COMFORT AND JOY,
COMFORT AND JOY! COMFORT AND JOY!
AH! AH! AH! AH! AH! AH! AH! AH!

*(Ruthie dies. Bat Boy bites the rabbit. Blood.)*

ALL.
AH AH AH AH!
AH AH AH AH!
AH AH AH AH AH AH,
AAAAAAHHH!!!

*(Blackout.)*

## ACT TWO

### Scene 1

*Revival tent. A cross. Spotlight on Reverend Hightower. He tries heroically to lift the spirits of the demoralized Hope Falls. This is an uphill battle.*

### "A JOYFUL NOISE"
**(Hightower, Ned, Bud, Maggie, Lorraine, Sheriff, Choir)**

REV. HIGHTOWER.
OH, THE SHEEP HAS RETURNED TO THE FOLD,
AND THE PRODIGAL SON HAS COME IN FROM THE COLD,
SO LIKE THE PROPHETS WERE TOLD IN THE DAYS OF OLD,
MAKE A JOYFUL NOISE, MY SOUL!!!
CHOIR.
*(Mumbling weakly.)*
… MAKE A JOYFUL NOISE, MY SOUL …

REV. HIGHTOWER.
OH, THE LION WILL LIE DOWN
WITH THE LAMB,

AND THE SINNER WILL WALK
HAND IN HAND WITH ABRAHAM,

AND HE WILL CRY TO THE SKY,
"JESUS, HERE I AM!"
MAKE A JOYFUL NOISE, MY SOUL!
*(Listening to Hightower, the Townsfolk miss their cue.)*
… HELLO?

MAKE SOME

TOWNSFOLK.

ON THAT
BRIGHT NEW
DAY …

HE WILL SHOW
THE WAY …

HERE I AM!

… FUL NOISE,
MY SOUL!
MAKE SOME

58

| | |
|---|---|
| NOISE! | NOISE! |
| MAKE SOME | MAKE SOME |
| NOISE! | NOISE! |
| MAKE SOME NOISE! | HALLELUJAH, |
| | MY SOUL IS |
| | WHOLE! |
| SING IT LOUD! | SING IT PROUD, |
| SING IT STRONG, | ALL NIGHT |
| | LONG! |
| MAKE A JOYFUL | MAKE SOME |
| NOISE, | NOISE, |
| A JOYFUL NOISE, | JOYFUL NOISE, |
| MY SOUL! | MY SOUL! |

All right, let's bring it down, let's bring it down. *(The band brings it down.)* I know there's someone out there. Someone who needs healing. I can feel your distress. You've got a sin … within! Step forward! Let the Holy Ghost heal you! The Holy Ghost is commanding you! He's putting a fire under your seat now. There's a fire under your seat. Mmmm now, feel it. No fear. Who wants the healing? *(Bat Boy, Meredith and Shelley enter, wearing their Sunday best. They stop just inside the entrance. The congregation gasps. Bat Boy steps forward. The music falters.)*

BAT BOY.  I want to be healed.

REV. HIGHTOWER.  *(Staring at him in horror.)* Oh, my Lord. Oh, Jesus, Son of God.

CONGREGATION.  *(Whispering.)* I can't believe it!/He showed up *here?*/We had an agreement.

REV. HIGHTOWER.  *(To congregation.)* Now, hold on, hold on. Let's bring it down, bring it down. *(They quiet down; to Bat Boy.)* You've got something bad in you, don't you, son?

BAT BOY.  Yes.

REV. HIGHTOWER.  And you want the healing.

BAT BOY.  Yes. I do.

REV. HIGHTOWER.  *(Beat.)* Well, come on down! *(Music. Bat Boy comes on down.)*

CROWD.  *(Ad-lib.)* Oh my Lordy! / This can't be happening. / I'm going to faint.

REV. HIGHTOWER.  Come on down, come on down! *(Bat Boy arrives.)* Well, look at you! You've got a hunger, don't you son? It's eating you up. It's gnawing a hole in your soul.

BAT BOY.  Yes.

REV. HIGHTOWER.  Are you ready for the healing? Are you ready for the healing?

BAT BOY. Yes. *(Bursts into tears.)* Yes! Yes! *(The preacher lays his hands on Bat Boy's head. He closes his eyes. He is deep in concentration. Music swells. Suddenly he opens his eyes and takes his hands off of Bat Boy's head. Music comes to a halt. He speaks very quietly.)*

REV. HIGHTOWER. I hear the Holy Ghost talking to me. He says there's someone in this room who doesn't want this boy to be healed. Can that be right? Is there someone here tonight who does not want healing for this boy? *(Dead silence. And more dead silence. Bat Boy looks out at the congregation.)*

BAT BOY. *(To congregation.)* I know … *(Clears throat.)* … I know you hate me. But I have to believe that it's because you don't know me. If you could see me … I mean, if you could really see me the way I see all of you …

## "LET ME WALK AMONG YOU"
### *(Bat Boy)*

BAT BOY.
> LOOK AT ALL YOUR FACES.
> CHILDREN, HUSBANDS, WIVES.
> GOD, YOU'RE ALL SO BEAUTIFUL.
> I ENVY YOU YOUR LIVES!
> GOING TO WORK,
> BUILDING YOUR SCHOOLS,
> THROWING A FOOTBALL
> OR SWIMMING IN POOLS,
> OUT IN THE SUN,
> LIVING BY RULES,
> I COULD LEARN HOW IF YOU'D TEACH ME THE TOOLS!
> I KNOW I'M STRANGE,
> SO HELP ME CHANGE.
> PLEASE,

> LET ME WALK AMONG YOU.
> LET ME SHOW MY FACE.
> I COULD LEARN TO LIVE WITH YOU,
> I CAN EARN MY PLACE.
> I WILL MOVE A MOUNTAIN;
> YOUR WISH IS MY COMMAND.

AND SOME DAY YOU MAY WANT TO SHAKE MY HAND.
I WILL PAINT YOUR HOUSES,
I'LL MILK YOUR COWS AT DAWN.
I WILL DO YOUR LAUNDRY,
AND I WILL MOW YOUR LAWN.
LET ME FILE YOUR TAXES.
I *AM* A CPA;
AND MAYBE THEN YOU'LL SHAKE MY HAND SOME DAY.

I CAN GROW A CHAMPION ROSE,
OR TEACH A YOGA CLASS,
I MYSELF DESIGNED THESE CLOTHES;
I CAN DO MY PART!
MUST I DIE THEN WITH MY NOSE
STILL PRESSED AGAINST THE GLASS? …
BUT IF YOU'D SHAKE MY HAND, WELL,
THAT'S A START,
YES, THAT'S A START,
LOOK IN YOUR HEART,
AND:
LET ME JOIN YOUR CARPOOL,
NO, LET ME DRIVE THE CAR,
LET ME THROW A BARBECUE,
OR JOIN YOU AT THE BAR.
COME AND WATCH THE BALLGAME,
I'LL BAKE A PECAN PIE.
AND I WILL SHAKE YOUR HAND WHEN YOU DROP BY.
OH, BRING ME TO YOUR CHURCHES,
AND LET ME LOOK INSIDE,
BRING ME TO YOUR WEDDINGS,
AND LET ME KISS THE BRIDE!
*(Long pause. Bat Boy realizes he's blown it. Very softly:)*
THANK YOU ALL FOR LISTENING.
THAT'S ALL I HAVE TO SAY …
*(He turns to leave, takes a few steps. He stops, turns back.)*
BUT PLEASE, WILL SOMEONE SHAKE MY HAND,
WON'T SOMEBODY TAKE MY HAND,
LET *JUST ONE PERSON* SHAKE MY HAND …

| ALL. | BAT BOY. |
|------|----------|

ALL.

  OKAY!

                         Okay?

  OKAY!

                         Okay?

  OKAY!

                         Okay?

  OKAYYY!

*(Rev. Hightower shakes Bat Boy's hand. They embrace. Gospel music. The entire congregation embraces and congratulates Bat Boy. Celebration.)*

ALL.

  PRAISE GOD, THE SHEEP HAS RETURNED TO THE FOLD,

  AND THE PRODIGAL SON HAS COME IN FROM THE COLD,

BAT BOY.

  SO LIKE THE PROPHETS WERE TOLD

BAT BOY AND TOWNSFOLK.

  IN THE DAYS OF OLD,

  MAKE A JOYFUL NOISE, MY SOUL,

  MAKE A JOYFUL NOISE, MY SOUL!

| BAT BOY. | TOWNSFOLK and REV. HIGHTOWER. |
|----------|-------------------------------|
| MAKE SOME NOISE | MAKE SOME NOISE! |
| MAKE SOME NOISE! | MAKE SOME NOISE! |
| MAKE SOME NOISE! | HALLELUJAH, |
| MY SOUL IS WHOLE! | MY SOUL IS WHOLE! |
| SING IT LOUD! | SING IT PROUD, |
| SING IT STRONG, | ALL NIGHT LONG! |

ALL.

  MAKE A JOYFUL NOISE,

  A JOYFUL NOISE MY SOUL,

  A JOYFUL NOISE MY SOUL,

  A JOYFUL NOISE MY SOUL,

  A JOYFUL NOISE

  MY SOUL!

  *AMEN!*

REV. HIGHTOWER. Amen! Amen! Thank you all for coming. God bless you. Our souls are full, but our bellies are empty, *(Moves to exit.)* so we have barbecue and lemonade outside. Praise Jesus! *(The Reverend exits swiftly. Parker enters, drunk.)* PARKER. There's something you all should know! *(Crowd turns to stare at him; he walks up the aisle to stage as crowd murmurs.)* I'm sorry, I'm sorry. I have some terrible news. Please, quiet down, I have some terrible news. It's about Edgar. *(Arrives at stage; sighs.)* I was working in my laboratory last night, studying a sample of Edgar's saliva. I made a startling discovery. This morning I rushed to the hospital to see if the state of Ruthie Taylor's wound confirmed my suspicions. Unfortunately, I discovered that Ruthie Taylor died in the night. *(Crowd gasps.)* Her death was due to a bizarre and unprecedented infection, an infection caused by Edgar's bite.

MEREDITH. No!

PARKER. I'm so sorry. Edgar is ... deadly. Deadly to Ruthie. And to cattle.

BUD. I knew it! He's the cause of the plague! *(Crowd murmur builds throughout the following.)*

PARKER. I'm sorry, Meredith.

BAT BOY. That girl is dead?

MEREDITH. *(To Bat Boy.)* It's not your fault, sweetheart. This must be a mistake.

PARKER. It's true, my love. It's true. I'm so sorry. I've called the Institute in Wheeling. They're coming to take him off our hands. *(Approaching her.)* I know it's difficult to accept all this, but we'll get through it together.

MEREDITH. *(Backing off.)* The Institute? This is madness.

BAT BOY. I never meant to hurt anybody.

PARKER. *(Still approaching her.)* Oh, sweetheart, I'll be here for you.

MEREDITH. What are you doing?

PARKER. Don't worry. Our love will get us through.

MEREDITH. Get your hands off me!

PARKER. That's right, let it out.

MEREDITH. *(To crowd.)* Please! Everyone! It's true Edgar was not civilized when he was first captured, but that's because he was a cornered animal back then. Since then ... I mean, look at him. You all just heard him. Can't you see that he's not a danger to any of us?

PARKER. Forgive her. She's taken to the boy! *(Enter Rick, Ron and Mrs. Taylor.)*

RICK. *(Going for Bat Boy.)* I'm gonna kill that freak!

MRS. TAYLOR. Ruthie's dead!!! He killed her! That freak killed my daughter!

BUD. *(Stopping Rick.)* Hang on there.

RON. Let me at him!

NED. Calm down, now.

BAT BOY. No, I didn't mean to.

NED. What're we doing now, Sheriff?

SHERIFF. We just gotta take a second ... .

MEREDITH. Thomas, why?

RICK. Murderer!

SHELLEY. Stop it, Rick.

MRS. TAYLOR. *(To Sheriff.)* You've got to do *something!*

RICK. Freak!

BAT BOY. I didn't know …

BUD. We can't let him roam free, Sheriff.

SHERIFF. I'm just saying let's take a second …

DAISY. This is terrible!

BAT BOY. No, I never meant to hurt anyone.

MRS. TAYLOR. You know what you have to do, Sheriff.

RICK. Animal!

SHELLEY. Stop it! *(Rick pulls out a pistol and fires it into the air. Everyone screams. The Sheriff pulls his revolver out and points it at Rick. Ad-lib hubbub.)*

SHERIFF. Now, don't do anything stupid, son.

MRS. TAYLOR. Don't you point a gun at my boy!

RICK. *(Waving gun around.)* Everyone shut up! *(To Bat Boy.)*
  I WANNA WATCH YOU WET YOUR PANTS TONIGHT,
  I'LL DIG YOUR GRAVE AND THEN I'LL DANCE TONIGHT.
  YOU WENT AND BLEW YOUR SECOND CHANCE TONIGHT!
*(To Townsfolk.)*
  ALL RIGHT? ALL RIGHT?
*(To Bat Boy.)*
  YOU SEE? I BROUGHT MY LOADED GUN TONIGHT.
  AND NOW YOU'LL PAY FOR WHAT YOU DONE TONIGHT.
  I GUESS THAT MEANS THE BEST MAN WON TONIGHT —
*(Before Rick can fire, Shelley steps in front of the gun.)*

SHELLEY.
  *RICK!* LEAVE THE BOY ALONE,
  PUT IT DOWN RIGHT NOW,
  YOU'RE AN *UGLY CREEP!*

*(Pause. Rick then roughly shoves Shelley away. Bat Boy grabs Rick by the shoulders, takes him down and bites his neck. When Bat Boy's face comes up again, it is covered in blood. Everyone gasps and moves back. Bat Boy runs away. Several townsfolk rush to Rick's body. Ad-lib hubbub. Bud picks up Rick's gun and fires three shots into the woods blindly. Meredith grabs Shelley by the hand and exits swiftly. Everyone yells at once. We make out the following lines:)*

SHERIFF. Bud, put that gun down right now!

BUD. I'm just helping.

SHERIFF. He's gone!

RON. Rick, are you all right?

BUD. *(Fires three more shots and hands gun to Sheriff.)* I think I might've winged him!

MRS. TAYLOR. My boy! My boy!

RICK. *(Very loud, shaking.)* Oh my God! Oh my God! *(Everyone quiets down and pays attention to Rick.)* Bat Boy bit me!

PARKER. *(Approaching Rick with his medical bag.)* Clear away, please!

MRS. TAYLOR. Dr. Parker, please save my boy. Please!

PARKER. *(Feels Rick's neck, prepares syringe.)* All right, Mrs. Taylor. Let's see what we can do here … *(Parker injects a fluid into Rick. Rick calms down, then convulses and dies just like Ruthie.)* I'm sorry. The wound was too deep. He's dead!

MRS. TAYLOR. My boy! First my daughter and now my boy! *(Mrs. Taylor and Ron kneel down over Rick's body.)*

TOWNSFOLK. Kill the freak!

RON. Rick? Wake up! Wake up, Rick …

MRS. TAYLOR. *(Pulling Ron close.)* Oh, Ronnie baby, don't you ever leave me, don't you ever leave your mama.

RON. Riiiiiiiiiick!!!!

BUD. Don't you worry, Mrs. Taylor, we'll find that critter.

SHERIFF. All right, folks! Listen up! Maggie, go call the ambulance, let's get this boy out of here. Lorraine, call the Institute and tell them to hurry up with that van! And somebody get some coffee into Dr. Parker, we need him. Now everybody else go home and get your guns and your dogs and get right back here. We're gonna do this right and orderly! All right now, move! We're losing time!

TOWNSFOLK. *(Enraged.)*
FIND THE BAT BOY,
STOP THE BAT BOY,
FIND THE BAT BOY,
STOP HIM!
FIND THE BAT BOY,
STOP THE BAT BOY,
FIND THE BAT BOY,
STOP THE …
… AAAAAHHH!!!!

*The woods. It is night. Meredith and Shelley hurry down a road that winds through the woods.*

MEREDITH.  Edgar!
SHELLEY.  Edgar! Oh, Edgar. Where are you? Mom, what are we going to do?

## "THREE-BEDROOM HOUSE"
### *(Meredith, Shelley)*

MEREDITH.
  OUT! OUT! OUT!
  TIME TO GET OUT!
  OUT!
  GOTTA JUST RIP OUT THIS PAGE,
  BEND THE BARS OF THE CAGE
  AND RUN FREE!
  FREE!
  NO ONE BUT EDGAR, YOU AND ME!
  GOTTA GO FIND HIM AND MOVE ON
  AND BE GONE
  BEFORE THE
  DAWN!
  GOTTA GET CHECKBOOKS,
  CAR KEYS,
  PASSPORTS,
  THEN GOODBYE!

  TOOTHBRUSH,
  BLANKETS,
  … NO.

Shelley, listen to me:

SHELLEY.

  Out?

  Free?

  AND BE GONE
  BEFORE THE
  DAWN!
  CHECKBOOKS,
  CAR KEYS,
  PASSPORTS,

  TOOTHBRUSH,
  BLANKETS,
  DADDY?

  Why?

WHAT DO YOU DO
WHEN YOU BLOW OUT A TIRE?                    Tire?
Trash it!
SOME HOLES YOU'LL NEVER PATCH!               You'll never
                                             patch? …

AND WHO DO YOU SAVE
WHEN YOUR HOUSE IS ON FIRE?                  Fire?
DON'T BRING THE GUY
WHO LIT THE MATCH!                           WHO LIT THE
                                             MATCH!

SO WE'LL GET A
POST OFFICE BOX,
AND WE'RE GONNA CHANGE
ALL THE LOCKS,
AND WE'RE GONNA STAY WITH
MY COUSINS A WHILE.
THEN WE'LL GET A
THREE-BEDROOM HOUSE
WITH A WHITE PICKET FENCE
AND A GUN AND A LAWYER,
SO SMILE!

GONNA GET A HOMEOWNER'S LOAN;                Could …
GONNA GET AN UNLISTED PHONE,                 Good! …
GONNA GET AWAY FROM A TOWN
GONE INSANE.                                 Kinda thought
                                             they would …

AND WE'LL GET A
THREE-BEDROOM HOUSE —                        A BEAUTIFUL
                                             THREE-BEDROOM
                                             HOUSE? …

AFFORDABLE
THREE-BEDROOM HOUSE …                         THREE-BEDROOM
                                             HOUSE …

WITH A GREAT BIG PIT BULL
ON A CHAIN!                                   *(Considering this.)*
                                             OKAY …
                                             OKAY, OKAY,
                                             OKAY, OKAY —

67

| | |
|---|---|
| | RIGHT! RIGHT!<br>RIGHT!<br>MOTHER, YOU'RE<br>RIGHT! |
| RIGHT? | |
| | RIGHT!<br>STILL KINDA<br>SAD THAT MY<br>DAD<br>LOST WHAT<br>MARBLES HE HAD,<br>BUT WE'RE FREE! |
| FREE! | |
| | FREE!<br>I'LL GET A<br>BRAND-NEW<br>FAKE ID! |
| AND IF WE LACK FOR ANYTHING,<br>I CAN HOCK THIS STUPID RING! | |
| AND WE'LL GET A<br>POST OFFICE BOX<br>AND WE'LL GET A<br>FRONT GATE<br>THAT LOCKS | AND WE'LL GET A<br>POST OFFICE BOX<br>AND WE'LL GET A<br>FRONT GATE<br>THAT LOCKS<br>AND WE'LL GET<br>AWAY<br>FROM THOSE<br>IGNORANT PIGS! |
| AND WE'LL GET A<br>THREE-BEDROOM<br>HOUSE,<br>A LIVABLE THREE-BEDROOM HOUSE, | AND WE'LL GET A<br>THREE-BEDROOM<br>HOUSE, |
| THREE-BEDROOM<br>HOUSE<br>AND SOME PLASTIC SURGERY<br>AND WIGS! | A LOVABLE<br>THREE-BEDROOM<br>HOUSE … |
| | *(Suspicious.)* |

For all of us! …


AND EDGAR
WILL SOON HAVE …


HIS OWN DRIVER'S LICENSE,


AND EDGAR
WILL SOON
HAVE
FIVE SUITS AND
A BRIEFCASE,


A GOOD DENTAL PLAN! …


YES, EDGAR WILL SOON HAVE
A HOME …

A HECK OF A
HOME! …
AND WE'LL GET A
POST OFFICE
BOX,
AND WE'LL GET A
FRONT GATE
 THAT LOCKS,
AND A BIG ELECTRIFIED FENCE
ALL AROUND!
AND WE'LL GET A
THREE-BEDROOM HOUSE —


NO HONEY,

For who? …

*(Satisfied.)*
Right!
AND EDGAR
WILL SOON HAVE
A GARDEN TO
WALK IN,

A CAR — NO,
A VAN!,
AND EDGAR
WILL SOON
HAVE …


A BALLROOM TO
DANCE IN,

'CAUSE EDGAR
WILL SOON HAVE
A HOME …
YES, EDGAR
WILL SOON HAVE
A HECK OF A
HOME! …
AND WE'LL GET A
POST OFFICE
BOX,
AND WE'LL GET A
FRONT GATE
THAT LOCKS,

WHOA!

OR EVEN A
TWO-BEDROOM
HOUSE.

A THREE-BEDROOM HOUSE —

Mom … Do you think Edgar would marry me?

*(Long pause.)*
NO HONEY A THREE-BEDROOM
HOUSE,
A THREE-BEDROOM HOUSE
IN A CONCRETE SHELTER
TEN FEET UNDERGROUND! —

SHELLEY. *(Grabbing Meredith's arm.)* MOM! I want to marry Edgar. I'm in love with him.

MEREDITH. No, Shelley.

SHELLEY. What?

MEREDITH. You're not in love with Edgar!

SHELLEY. Yes, I am. Mom, I love him so much. And I want to be with him forever —

MEREDITH. No, Shelley! Absolutely not! That's a horrible thing to say. Don't say that again!

SHELLEY. Mother!

MEREDITH. It's hideous. It's not right!

SHELLEY. *(Shocked.)* You're just like the rest of them.

MEREDITH. *(Grabbing Shelley.)* You don't understand — *(Shelley shoves her away. Meredith falls. Shelley flees into the woods.)* Shellllleeeeey! *Nooooooooooooooo!* …
WHAT ABOUT THE THREE-BEDROOM HOUSE?
THE THREE-BEDROOM HOUSE? …
WHO DO YOU SAVE WHEN YOUR HOUSE IS ON FIRE …
YOUR HOUSE IS ON FIRE …
YOUR HOUSE IS ON *FIRE!!!*

# Scene 3

*A clearing in the woods. Shelley enters.*

SHELLEY.  Edgar! Edgar! Oh, where are you? Oh, Edgar. *(Bat Boy suddenly appears. He touches Shelley's shoulder. She is startled, then she hugs him.)* You found me! How did you find me?

BAT BOY.  I see very well in this light.

SHELLEY.  *(Crying.)* Oh, Edgar, we've got to get away. They're coming after you and I'm worried what they're going to do, and my mother, she ... *(She pulls a handkerchief from her pocket and wipes her tears. Bat Boy stares at her. When she looks back up at Bat Boy, she sees that he is crying as well. She hands him her handkerchief.)* Here.

BAT BOY.  Thank you. *(Bat Boy dries his tears. He moves to hand back the handkerchief.)*

SHELLEY.  No, you can keep it. It's a gift.

BAT BOY.  Oh. Thank you. *(When their hands touch, music starts. Shelley and Bat Boy look at each other. We hear a disembodied voice:)*

## "CHILDREN, CHILDREN"
### *(Pan, Animals, Bat Boy, Shelley)*

PAN.
*(Offstage.)*
  CHILDREN, WELCOME HOME,
  TO WHERE WE ALL BEGAN.
  ALONE AND FACE TO FACE
  LET US ERASE THE FALL OF MAN ...
*(Enter the god Pan.)*
  NOW LET THE FROGS PAUSE IN THEIR SONG,
  NOW LET THE CRICKETS HOLD THEIR BREATH;
  NOW LET THE TREES STAND STILL AS DEATH
  AND TELL THE MOSQUITOES NOT TO BITE.
  NOW WE'VE BEEN HOPING FOR SO LONG,
  SO FILL THE SKY WITH FIREFLIES.

SO THEY CAN SEE INTO EACH OTHER'S EYES
AND THEN THEY'LL GET IT RIGHT …
*(Animals enter and investigate Bat Boy and Shelley.)*

OH, CHILDREN, CHILDREN, DON'T BE SCARED.
THE MOON IS UP AND WE'RE ALL PREPARED.
CHILDREN, TAKE A LOOK AROUND,
WE'RE ON SACRED GROUND —
AND WHAT WE THOUGHT WAS LOST AT LAST IS FOUND.

| | THE ANIMALS. |
|---|---|
| NOW LET THE TURTLE AND THE DOVE, | OOH, SHA LA LA! |
| LET THE LION AND THE LAMB, | OOH, SHA LA LA! |
| LET THE OWL AND WOLF AND | |
| RAM EMBRACE | OOOH, SHA LA LA! |
| ACROSS THE COUNTRYSIDE, | ACROSS THE |
| | COUNTRYSIDE! |
| FUR AND FEATHERS MAKING LOVE, | OOH, SHA LA LA! |
| PAWS AND CLAWS AND JAWS | |
| AND BEAKS. | OOH, AAAH, |
| | SHA LA LA! |
| LET THE SONG GO ON | OOH, AAAH … |
| FOR WEEKS AND WEEKS | |
| TO BLESS THIS BOY | BLESS THIS BOY |
| AND | AND |
| BLESS THIS | BLESS THIS |
| BRIDE! | BRIDE! |

PAN and ANIMALS.
    OH, CHILDREN, CHILDREN, DON'T BE SCARED.
    THE MOON IS UP AND WE'RE ALL PREPARED.
    CHILDREN, TAKE A LOOK AROUND,
    HEAR THAT JOYFUL SOUND —
    FOR WHAT WE THOUGHT WAS LOST AT LAST IS FOUND.
    SHA LA LA LA LA LA!
    THE EARTH'S ASLEEP, TIME TO WAKE IT.
    IF YOU HAVE CLOTHING, FORSAKE IT.
    WE WANT YOU BREATHLESS AND NAKED!
    CHOOSE YOUR MATE;
    AND THEN LET'S SEE WHAT WE CREATE! …

*HEY!*

*(Dance break — animals copulate in various combinations. At some point Bat Boy and Shelley exit. They reappear, naked, demurely covering their sensitive areas with foliage. Pan presides over a sort of marriage ceremony.)*

PAN.

DRAW NEAR, MY DEARLY BELOVED,
NO PRIEST, NO CHURCH, BUT WHAT
OF IT?
TAKE ROOT, TAKE FLIGHT, I
COMMAND IT,
HERE WE STAND,
SO NO MORE STALLING,
TAKE HER HAND!
OH,
CHILDREN, CHILDREN,
DON'T BE SCARED!

THE MOON IS UP
AND WE'RE ALL PREPARED.
CHILDREN, TAKE A LOOK AROUND,
WE'RE ON SACRED GROUND,

AND HEAR THAT JOYFUL SOUND! —
FOR WHAT WE THOUGHT WAS,
WHAT WE THOUGHT WAS

LOST —
AT LAST IS
FOUND!
FOUND!
FOUND!
FOUND!

THE ANIMALS.

AAAH, AAH, AAH!

AAAH, AAH, AAH!

AAAH, AAH, AAH!
HERE WE STAND,

CHILDREN!
DON'T BE
SCARED.

ALL PREPARED!
TAKE A LOOK
AROUND! SHA
LA LA!
'OUND, SHA LA LA,

WHAT WE
THOUGHT WAS
LOST —
AT LAST IS
FOUND!
FOUND!
FOUND!
FOUND!

*(The animals surround Bat Boy and Shelley in celebration.)*

# Scene 4

*Another area of the woods. Enter Ron.*

RON. I'm gonna get you Bat Boy! You'll pay for what you did to Rick and Ruthie. You hear me, freak! You're gonna pay! *(Ron runs through the woods.)* Wait a second. The freak digs blood, right? And where do they have the most blood in Hope Falls? *(Lights up on the slaughterhouse.)* The *slaughterhouse!* He's in the slaughterhouse! I'm gonna get you, Bat Boy! Aaaaaah! *(Screaming, Ron runs into the slaughterhouse. But he can still be heard screaming and throwing things around. Enter Daisy with torch and walkie-talkie.)*

DAISY. *(Whispering.)* Sweet Jesus! *(To walkie-talkie.)* Fox Leader, this is Henhouse. You copy? Over.

SHERIFF'S VOICE. *(On walkie-talkie.)* Daisy? Is that you?

DAISY. *(To walkie-talkie.)* Ten-four. I'm at the slaughterhouse, and there's some kind of a ruckus going on in there. I think it might be the Bat Boy. Over.

SHERIFF'S VOICE. *(On walkie-talkie.)* All right, Daisy. You hold on until we get there. You understand me? Don't do *anything*. The Institute Man will be here soon and he'll take care of it.

DAISY. *(To walkie-talkie.)* That's a big ten-four affirmative, Fox Leader. Over and out. Sweet Jesus! *(Mrs. Taylor comes running on, hysterical.)*

MRS. TAYLOR. Have you seen Ron? Have you seen my baby?

DAISY. You best stay back, Mrs. Taylor. We got the Bat Boy trapped inside the slaughterhouse.

MRS. TAYLOR. The Bat Boy is in there?

DAISY. I think so.

MRS. TAYLOR. And you're just standing here? *(Mrs. Taylor suddenly grabs Daisy's torch right out of her hand. She runs to the slaughterhouse entrance ... )* Burn, Bat Boy! Burn! *( ... and throws the torch through the door. Whoosh!!! The slaughterhouse ignites. We hear a scream from inside.)*

DAISY. Oh, my Lordie. *(Sound of hounds. Enter Sheriff, Ned and Mr. Dillon. Everyone stares at the burning slaughterhouse, stunned.)*

SHERIFF. What the —

DAISY. Don't look at me. She burned him up!

MR. DILLON. There he is! *(The figure of Ron on fire [or just crispy and smoking] suddenly appears at the door and takes a few steps out. He isn't recognizable. The*

74

*Sheriff runs to Ron, throws his coat around him and tackles him to the ground. Mrs. Taylor runs over to them and points her finger.)*

MRS. TAYLOR. That's right. Burn, you freak! Burn. You'll pay for what you did to me. You'll pay in hell, Bat Boy.

RON. Mom? *(Mrs. Taylor's jaw drops. She falls to her knees.)*

MRS. TAYLOR. AAAAAAAAAAAAAAAAAAAAAAHHHHHHHHHHHH!!!!!!!!!!!!!
*(Ron dies.)* First my daughter and then my son and now my baby! *(Enter Parker, displaying syringe.)*

PARKER. Okay! Clear away! Let's see what we can do here.

MRS. TAYLOR. Dr. Parker. Please save my baby! Please!

PARKER. *(Approaches Ron with a syringe at the ready and feels his neck.)* All right, Mrs. Taylor. Let's — oh … he's dead.

MRS. TAYLOR. AAAAAAAAAAAAAAAAAAAAAAHHHHHHHHHHHH!!!!!!!!!!!!!
Sheriff, you've got to find that Bat freak and kill it. You've got to make him pay for this!

SHERIFF. Oh, Lordy!, I wish that Institute Man would hurry it up. *(To walkie-talkie.)* Bud, this is the Sheriff. You there?

BUD'S VOICE. Ten-four. I'm positioned on the highway at the town limits. Over.

SHERIFF. That's great, Bud. You let me know as soon as you see any sign of the van from the Institute, okay?

BUD'S VOICE. That's an affirmative, Fox Leader. Ten-four, over and out.

MAGGIE. Sheriff — what are we going to do? That Bat Boy could swoop down on us any minute!

CROWD. *(Ad-lib hubbub.)* Oh my Lordy! / That's right! / We're all in danger.

SHERIFF. All right, everybody. Pipe down! *(Pulling Parker aside.)* Dr. Parker, we've got a mob forming here. Is there anything you can do to calm these people down?

PARKER. Certainly, Sheriff. Happy to do it. *(To crowd.)* Don't worry folks, the creature is on what is commonly known as a "rampage." You see, love has been shown to him, then taken away. Like a dog beaten once too often by its mistress, he has turned on her and all humans. Nothing will slake his thirst. His wrath will spare no one.

MORE BLOOD WILL BE SPILT.
HUNGER HAS INCREASED.
NOTHING LEFT OF GUILT.
BEAST HAS BEEN RELEASED!
DAMN THE WORLD OF MEN!
EVERYONE WILL PAY!
*I SHALL KILL AGAIN!*

*(Parker freezes, realizing he's holding his syringe aloft and everyone is staring at him. His eyes dart about.)* Um … er, uh … uh,

*THAT'S WHAT HE WOULD SAY!*
*(The Townsfolk go nuts.)*
TOWNSFOLK.
  FIND THE BAT BOY!
  KILL THE BAT BOY!
  FIND HIM! KILL HIM!
  FIND HIM! KILL HIM!
  FIND! KILL! FIND! KILL!
  FIND! KILL! FIND! KILL! …
  AAAAAAAAAAAHHHH!


## Scene 5


*Clearing. Shelley and Bat Boy cuddle peacefully, semi-clothed. The animals are gone.*


SHELLEY.  I wish we could stay like this forever.
BAT BOY.  I've never felt like this.
SHELLEY.  How do you feel?
BAT BOY.  I feel … complete. *(Beat.)* Also I feel hungry.
SHELLEY.  Oh.
BAT BOY.  Shelley, there's something I have to tell you.
SHELLEY.  It's okay.
BAT BOY.  No, I wouldn't feel right not —
SHELLEY.  I know. *(Looks at Bat Boy.)* I know.


### "INSIDE YOUR HEART"
### *(Bat Boy, Shelley)*


SHELLEY.
  IT'S OKAY.
  I'M STILL HERE.
  YOUR SECRET'S OUT, BUT DON'T FEAR.
  'CAUSE I DON'T CARE WHAT PEOPLE SAY.

ONCE I THOUGHT YOU WERE WEIRD;
BUT SOON MY DOUBTS DISAPPEARED.
I THINK YOU'RE NORMALLER THAN THEY.
NOW YOU'RE SCARED;
YOU'RE IN NEED;
CLEARLY SOMEONE HAS TO BLEED.
I'LL REPAY ALL YOU GAVE;
I WILL GIVE YOU WHAT YOU CRAVE.
*(Shelley holds out her arm, offering it to Bat Boy. He is shocked.)*
LET ME PROVE I LOVE YOU,
LET ME BECOME PART OF YOU.
I SEE NO BETTER WAY TO START:
NOW I CAN LIVE INSIDE YOUR HEART.

SHELLEY.

BAT BOY.
YOU DON'T KNOW WHAT
YOU'RE SAYING —

YES I DO —

GO ON, GO HOME, FORGET
ME —

IT'S FOR YOU —

I'LL HURT YOU, I'M NOT
PLAYING —

NO, I KNEW THAT
WHEN I —

PLEASE DON'T

LET ME —

LET ME —
NO!

I WANT TO,
PLEASE —
YES!

PLEASE —

NO!, IT'S TOO BIZARRE —

JUST —

JUST —
GO!

I'M NOT AFRAID,
IT'S NO DISEASE,
IT'S WHO YOU ARE —

IT MURDERS
EVERYTHING
I TOUCH,
A SCREAMING FIRE WILL

77

FILL YOU,
YOU'LL BEG ME PLEASE TO
KILL YOU —
I COULD NOT LET YOU BE
MY CRUTCH,
OH, GOD, I FEEL MY HUNGER
GROW —
*GO!* GO ON, GO HOME,
FORGET ME …

*(Snorting.)*
    NO.
    SUCH A LOVELY BOY,
    LOOK AT WHAT YOU'VE DONE TO ME,
    WOKE ME UP AND SET ME FREE,
    SO LOOK AT ME;
    SUCH A LOVELY BOY,
    THIS WAY YOU'LL BE MINE AT LAST;
    AND I'LL BE FINE: I HEAL REAL FAST.
    SO LOOK AT ME …
    LOOK AT ME! …
BAT BOY.
    YOU DON'T KNOW WHAT YOU'RE SAYING —
SHELLEY.
    SHUT UP, THAT'S IT, I'M STAYING! …
SHELLEY and BAT BOY.
    I WILL SHIELD YOU FROM HARM;
    COME SPEND YOUR LIFE ON MY ARM.
    I SEE NO BETTER WAY TO START.
    LET ME PROVE I LOVE YOU;
    LET ME BECOME PART OF YOU.
    NOW WE SHALL NEVER BE APART.
    I'LL ALWAYS LIVE INSIDE YOUR HEA …
*(Catching breath.)*
    … EART!
BAT BOY.  I love you, Shelley.
SHELLEY.  I love you, Edgar. *(Bat Boy lowers his head to Shelley's arm. Enter Meredith. She stands in shock.)*
MEREDITH.  NNNOOOOOOOOO!!!
SHELLEY.  *(Covering herself.)* Mother!

MEREDITH. Abomination! Get away from him! *(To Bat Boy.)* Get away from her!

SHELLEY. I love him, Mother!

MEREDITH. *(Grabbing Shelley and pulling her away.)* This is an abomination!

BAT BOY. *(Still shaking.)* We're in love.

MEREDITH. That's not possible! I won't hear it!

SHELLEY. And I won't hear you call Edgar an abomination!

MEREDITH. You don't understand!

SHELLEY. You don't love him! You can't love him! If you loved him you wouldn't want to keep us from each other!

MEREDITH. Please, sweetheart, don't speak of it. I can't stand it.

SHELLEY. He's not a freak, Mother. He's a decent, loving, passionate boy and I love him and I want to be with him for the rest of my life!

MEREDITH. Stop! You must understand how hideous that sounds!

BAT BOY. Mrs. Parker! Why do you hate me so?

MEREDITH. I don't hate you. Oh, dear Edgar.

BAT BOY. It's because of you that I can love Shelley …

MEREDITH. No!

BAT BOY. … how can you wish to take that from me? *(Moves toward Meredith menacingly.)* Is all that you taught me a lie? Is it only from a distance that I am your dear, sweet Edgar? But when I get too close I'm a *freak!*

MEREDITH. No!

BAT BOY. *(Moves close.)* A *menace!*

MEREDITH. No!

BAT BOY. *(Closer, losing it.)* An *abomination!*

MEREDITH. *(Cowering.)* No!

BAT BOY. You'll not keep us apart! I'll do what I must! *(Bat Boy lunges, bringing Meredith to the ground.)*

SHELLEY. Edgar, no!

BAT BOY. *(Bares his fangs.)* I'll do what I must!

MEREDITH. Edgar! I'm your *mother!* I'm your mother. *(Bat Boy recoils. A long beat, then Meredith sobs.)* I'm so sorry. I didn't see this. I'm so sorry. My own dear Edgar.

BAT BOY. No.

MEREDITH. Oh, my Edgar. *(Bat Boy and Shelley regard each other, shamed. The sound of approaching hounds.)*

BAT BOY. *(Running off.)* Noooooooooo!

MEREDITH. *(To Shelley.)* Honey, please, come to me. Come here, sweetheart … *(Shelley opens her mouth as if to scream in horror. But we hear the sound of a cow being killed.)*

## Scene 6

*At the mouth of the cave. Bat Boy enters screaming. He holds a severed cow head in his hands.*

## "APOLOGY TO A COW"
### (Bat Boy)

BAT BOY.
    I'M SORRY, FRIEND, I HAVE TO.
    I KNOW, I KNOW IT'S RUDE.
    I SHOULDN'T WORK MY PROBLEMS OUT WITH
    FOOD.
    I'M SORRY PAL, I'VE GOT TO.
    IT'S EITHER ME OR YOU.
    FIGHT OR BE BEATEN.
    EAT OR BE EATEN.
    LOOK WHAT IT MAKES ME DO.
    IT'S STRONGER THAN IT WAS,
    AND THIS IS WHAT THE BAT CHILD DOES.
*(Bat Boy sinks to his knees, utterly defeated.)*

    DEEP IN THE CAVE UNDER MILES OF STONE,
    I KNEW NO WORD FOR SAD.
    SINGING TO ECHOES AND ALL ALONE,
    NEEDED NO MOM OR DAD.
    I'D NEVER DREAMED OF THE WORLD ABOVE;
    I'D NEVER SEEN THE SKY.
    AND YET I WAS CONTENT;
    I NEVER WONDERED WHY.

    I NEVER KNEW SUCH A WORD AS "RAGE,"
    I LEARNED THAT FROM *YOU.*
    YOU LOCKED YOUR BOY UP INSIDE A CAGE,
    AND ALL OF THE WHILE *YOU KNEW!*

*WHY* BOTHER GIVING ME DAD'S OLD SHIRT,
*WHY* EVEN INTERVENE?
*WHY* BOTHER WASHING OFF ALL THE DIRT,
IF I AM STILL UNCLEAN?
YOU SAID YOU'D NEVER HURT ME, MOM,
WHATEVER MIGHT OCCUR!,
*SO:*

HOW COULD YOU DARE, MOM,
MAKE ME "AWARE," MOM,
TEACH ME TO CARE, MOM,
AND THEN DENY ME *HER!!!* ...

WE HAD A CHANCE AT HAPPINESS,
BLISSFULLY UNAWARE ...
WE HAD A LOVE WE THOUGHT YOU'D BLESS,
WE NEVER HAD A PRAYER!
CAUSE *YOU* HAD TO COME DESTROY OUR LOVE
LIKE *EVERYTHING ELSE* I HAD!
YET *STILL I AM CONTENT*
AND I AM *NOT THE LEAST BIT MAD* ...
NO, I'M NOT HERE TO HARM YOU;
I ONLY WANT TO *KILL!!!*

| BAT BOY. | SCARY CHORUS. |
|---|---|
| YOU SHALL HAVE YOUR MONSTER, | |
| I SHALL DRINK MY FILL! | |
| *(Bat Boy climbs and hangs upside down.)* | |
| AT LAST I AM EMBRACING | |
| MY BLOODY DESTINY! | AHH ... |
| DEAR MOM AND DAD, THIS FACE | |
| WILL BE ... | AHH ... |
| THE *LAST THING* THAT YOU *EVER SEE!* | AHH ... |
| *(Bat Boy leaps down.)* | |
| *REVENGE* WILL BE A HOME FOR ... | *AAHH!* |
| *ME!!!* | AH AH AH! AH |
| | AH AH! |
| FOR *ME!!!* | AH AH AH! |
| FOR ... | AH AH AH! |

81

MEEEEEEE!!!                                    AAAHH!!!

*(Bat Boy brings the cow head to his mouth and feeds. We hear the sound of hounds. Parker enters with Ned and Roy. Parker motions Ned and Roy, who both carry shotguns, around to opposite sides of the stage to cover Bat Boy.)*

NED. *(Stares at Bat Boy; in shock.)* That's Gertie. My Lord, he's killed Gertie.

ROY. *(Aiming shotgun.)* That does it! Someone's got to kill this thing.

NED. *(Still in shock.)* Oh, Gertie …

BAT BOY. Hello, Father.

ROY. What's he talking about, Dr. Parker?

PARKER. What has she told you?

BAT BOY. Enough. What have I ever done to lose the favor of my father? Tell me!

PARKER. You're not my son!

BAT BOY. Do you want to die with that lie on your lips? *(Bat Boy takes a step toward Parker.)*

ROY. Stand back, Dr. Parker! *(Enter Sheriff.)*

SHERIFF. Hold on! Nobody's shooting anybody here. Stand down, Roy. What do you think you're doing, Edgar? *(Enter Maggie, Lorraine and Bud.)*

BAT BOY. I'm going to kill my father.

PARKER. I'm not your father! *(All react.)*

NED. That does it! Somebody's got to kill this thing!

CROWD. *(Angry hubbub.)* That's right! / Do it, Ned! / Shoot him! *(Enter Meredith with Shelley.)*

MEREDITH. Stop! All of you! Please don't hurt my son!

SHELLEY. Edgar!

TOWNSFOLK. What's she talking about?/She's his mother?/That's impossible!/Who's his father?

MEREDITH. Please, just stop. If you would only listen to his story, you'd understand. Please let me tell you his story! *(To Parker.)* For God's sake, Thomas, let's just tell the truth — for once and for all, we must get this secret out.

PARKER. *(Beat.)* I should have done as you told me on the day he was born. *(All react.)* Or don't you remember?

MEREDITH. I remember everything. *(Lights out. Angry music. Sound effect of a baby crying. The voice of a younger Meredith comes out over the speakers: "Kill it! Kill it!" Lights up on Meredith and Parker. They wear lab coats and hold test tubes. Bat Boy and Shelley watch the scene from the shadows. They are looking in on the other characters' memories and cannot participate. Meredith and Parker talk directly to the audience.)* I was Thomas' assistant at the time.

PARKER. I was a young and ambitious vet just starting out.

MEREDITH. I loved him dearly.

PARKER.  I loved her dearly. I hoped that she would marry me if I asked.
MEREDITH.  I was hoping he would ask me to marry him.

| MEREDITH. | PARKER. |
|---|---|
| AND THERE WAS<br>A TIME OR TWO<br>WHEN HE HAD<br>DANCED WITH<br>ME, | AND THERE WAS<br>A TIME OR TWO<br>WHEN SHE HAD<br>DANCED WITH<br>ME,<br>HER SKIN WAS<br>SO SOFT. |
| HE WAS GORGEOUS AND YOUNG.<br>AND I WOULD<br>MELT IN HIS ARMS,<br>WE DANCED FIVE HOURS<br>OR MORE, | AND SHE WOULD<br>MELT IN MY ARMS,<br><br>BUT WE WOULD<br>PART AT HER<br>DOOR, |

MEREDITH and PARKER.
  AND WE KISSED WITH NO TONGUE.
  WE'D MADE A PROMISE TO WAIT,
  AND IT WAS GONNA BE GREAT.

PARKER.  *(Raising a test tube.)* I was developing a pheromone to increase birth yield in cattle.
MEREDITH.  It would have been a windfall for him if it had been successful.
PARKER.  We were working late one night in my laboratory.
MEREDITH.  And that's when the accident happened. *(Parker spills the contents of the test tube on Meredith. Parker and Meredith talk to each other.)*
PARKER.  *(Cleaning the spill off of Meredith's lab coat.)* I'm so sorry.
MEREDITH.  It's all right.
PARKER.  I'm such a klutz.
MEREDITH.  It's not a problem, really.
PARKER.  *(To audience.)* The pheromone was designed to be rubbed into the hide of the cow to stimulate sexual arousal in the bull.
MEREDITH.  *(To audience.)* But he'd had no success with his experiments. In desperation, he explored beyond the bounds of accepted scientific practice. *(Parker sniffs the air.)* Into the bovine solution, he introduced the pheromones of a dozen other animals. Some endangered. Some human. The result had properties greater, and more universal, than he had intended.
PARKER.  *(Grabs Meredith.)* You are so beautiful. *(He kisses her roughly.)*

MEREDITH. *(To Parker.)* Dr. Parker! What are you doing?

PARKER. Love me, Meredith.

MEREDITH. Thomas, no!

PARKER.
DANCE WITH ME, DARLING,
DANCE WITH ME, DARLING,
LOVE ME, LOVE ME, MEREDITH!

MEREDITH.
Thomas, no!

PARKER.
LOVE ME!

*(Parker lifts Meredith onto the table and begins roughly loving her. He suddenly shifts to slow motion as Meredith speaks.)*

MEREDITH. *(To audience.)* To say that he took me would be romanticizing the act. To say that he raped me would be unfair. He was beyond his own control, acting on an impulse of his own creation that I'm sure he didn't understand. It was the most painful experience I had had in my young life ... But, of course, I had no idea what was about to happen as I tried to walk back home. *(Lights out. Shadow Play: Young Meredith walks home sobbing. A bat flutters by too close to her head. She ducks. The bat returns and attaches itself to her dress. She struggles to pull it off. Another bat flies on and attaches itself, then another, and another. Young Meredith runs off screaming. Lights up center stage: Young Meredith, covered head to toe in bats, writhes uncontrollably. She screams. Lights up on Meredith.)* The bats were attracted by the pheromone. They were everywhere. They bit, they burrowed — they burrowed ... everywhere. They violated me. I ran. They followed me as I ran for home. I hoped my parents would know what to do.

FATHER. *(Offstage.)* Dear God! Meredith!

MOTHER. *(Offstage.)* What's going on? — Oh my Lord!

FATHER. *(Offstage.)* Bats! Help me get them off her.

MEREDITH. I felt the bats release. Were they done with me? Was this horror finally over? I looked up. The bats went after my parents. *(Parker enters.)*

PARKER. The next morning, I found Meredith barely alive between the dead bodies of her parents. I took her to my home. I still loved her, though we were both so ashamed that we couldn't even look at each other. When I discovered, two months after the incident, that Meredith was pregnant with my child, I begged her to marry me. I hoped that she would love me again.

MEREDITH. In my heart, I knew that I could never love him again, but I wanted my child to have a father.

PARKER. We moved to Hope Falls, where I was sure with time we could put the horrors of the past behind us. But the true horror was yet to come. *(Lights out.*

*Shadow Play: Young Meredith's legs up in the air. She is huffing and puffing.)*

DOCTOR #2. Just one more push. That's it. Good. Wonderful. Congratulations Meredith, you are the mother of a baby girl.

YOUNG MEREDITH. She's beautiful. Can I hold her?

DOCTOR #2. Let's just clean her off for you and we'll … wait a second, what's this? Hang on.

YOUNG MEREDITH. *(In pain.)* Ahh! What is it?

DOCTOR #2. Give me one more little push would you, Meredith? There seems to be … something else —

YOUNG MEREDITH. *(Pushing.)* What is it?

DOCTOR #2. I'm not sure. May just be the placenta — oh, my God! *(We hear the bat cries, and the Doctor holds up a small wriggling bat baby.)*

| YOUNG MEREDITH. | ALL. |
|---|---|
| | AH! AH! AH! AH! |
| KILL IT! | AH AH! |
| KILL IT! | AH AH! |
| *KILL IIIIT!* | *AHHHH!* |

*(Lights out on the shadow play. Lights up on Parker carrying a bundle and a shovel.)*

PARKER. The job fell to me. I took the bat child out to the woods. I had put to sleep countless animals in my work, so killing the thing should not have been a problem. I dearly hoped that this act would finally convince Meredith of the depth of my love for her. *(Parker sets the bundle on the ground; he raises the shovel to kill the thing.)* But I found that I couldn't do it. I felt, to my horror, that I would be killing my own creation. Nonetheless, I couldn't take such a monster back into my home, to my wife, and have it serve as a reminder of the past we'd worked so hard to erase. *(Picks up the bundle.)* So I left you at the mouth of a cave, certain that time or predators would do what I couldn't do myself. *(Sets the bundle at the front of the shadow-play screen.)* But I was wrong …

| PARKER. | ALL but BAT BOY. |
|---|---|
| THE BATS, | |
| YOUR TRUE FATHERS, | |
| CAME AND THEY TOOK YOU, | |
| DOWN TO THEIR MIDNIGHT LAIRS, | |
| THE BATS, YOUR TRUE FATHERS, | THE BATS, YOUR TRUE FATHERS, |
| CLAIMED YOU — | CLAIMED YOU — |

PARKER and MEREDITH. … And made you theirs.

ALL but BAT BOY.

AH AH AH AH, AH AH AH AH, AH!

*(Lights out. Shadow play: Bats flutter behind the screen. Lights up on the present.)*
BAT BOY. *(To Parker.)* I wish you had not been a coward.
MEREDITH. *(To the crowd.)* So you see, he's not a beast. He's my son. He's just a misunderstood boy. He's one of us. Please …
BUD. But he's the cause of the plague!
MEREDITH. There is no plague, Bud! You're trying to raise cows on the side of a mountain!
SHELLEY. Edgar, we can still be a family.
BAT BOY. You were right, Mother, to have wanted me dead. It wasn't a crime to have wished death upon me. Your crime was in giving me hope. How could you tell me I was human, when you knew me to be a beast?
NED. Should I kill him?
MEREDITH. You're not a beast. Could a beast speak as eloquently as you?
LORRAINE. Kill the freak!
BAT BOY. What good is eloquence, when I can only use it to answer taunts and jeers?
MAGGIE. Shoot him, Ned!
MEREDITH. Look inside yourself, Edgar, and you'll see a soul. Does a beast have a soul?
BAT BOY. A "soul"?


## "FINALE: I IMAGINE YOU'RE UPSET"
### *(Bat Boy, Shelley, Meredith, Parker, Sheriff, Townsfolk)*


BAT BOY.
　　IS THAT WHAT YOU CALL IT, THAT EMPTY PIT,
　　THAT *WOUND* WHERE MY HEART SHOULD BE?
　　*YOU* DUG THIS HOLE IN ME BIT BY BIT,
　　NOTHING IS LEFT OF ME.
　　GIVE ME ONE REASON WHY I SHOULD LIVE!
　　SEE? YOU HAVE NO REPLY.
　　THE WORLD IS MAN OR BEAST,
　　BUT I AM BOTH AND NEITHER.
　　SO GOODBYE!
*(Bat Boy walks with arms open toward Ned's rifle. The Sheriff steps between them.)*
SHERIFF.
　　I'M SORRY, EDGAR, REALLY AM.

SORRY TO HEAR YOUR LIFE'S A SHAM.
STILL IT DOESN'T HAVE TO END THIS WAY! …
*(Holding out handcuffs.)*
SO PUT THESE ON AND DON'T BE CUTE.
A VAN'S EN ROUTE FROM THE INSTITUTE.
HE GETS IN IT, NO ONE DIES TODAY!.
Back off, people!
MOB.
SHERIFF YOU IDIOT,
WHY DO YOU PITY IT?
LOOK AT THE BLOOD ON HIM,
WHY DON'T YOU KILL HIM!

| BAT BOY. | MOB. |
|---|---|
| DON'T DENY THE OBVIOUS. | GRAB HIM! |
| SUCH AN UGLY BOY. | GET HIM! |
| EVERYWHERE YOU PUT ME, | |
| LOOK WHAT I DESTROY. | |

*(Bat Boy pulls the knife from Parker's belt. The mob reacts. Bat Boy turns the knife around and hands it to Parker.)*
BAT BOY.
NOT STRUNG UP BY FARMERS,
OR CAGED IN BY POLICE.
IF YOU'RE NOT A COWARD,
GIVE ME PEACE.
MOB.
PARKER YOU IDIOT,
WHY DO YOU PITY IT?
LOOK AT THE BLOOD ON HIM,
WHY DON'T YOU KILL HIM!
*(Parker can't do it.)*
BAT BOY.  Coward.
PARKER.  I'm sorry. *(Bat Boy sighs. Parker has left him no choice:)*
BAT BOY.  You know …

| BAT BOY. | SHELLEY. | MEREDITH. |
|---|---|---|
| ONE THING ALONE | | |
| SAVED ME FROM DESPAIR, | | |
| BACK IN MY FERAL STAGE. | EDGAR … | |
| ONCE IN A WHILE SHE | | |
| WOULD MEET MY STARE. | | |
| THEN I'D FORGET THE CAGE. | | EDGAR, DON'T! |

SURELY HER SMILE WASN'T
MEANT FOR ME.                          EDGAR, NO!
EASIER TO DISMISS.
BUT, TONIGHT SHE
KISSED ME, HERE.
*(General shock. Bat Boy takes one last look at Shelley.)*
BAT BOY.
   TONIGHT SHE GAVE ME THIS.
*(He produces Shelley's handkerchief. General perplexity.)*

BAT BOY.                          PARKER.          TOWNSFOLK.
*(Partly to himself.)*
   I SMELL HER PERFUME
   AND HER SWEAT …                 OH MY
                                   GOD …          JESUS! …

*(To the crowd.)*
   LOOK WHAT A GIFT SHE
   GAVE ME.                        IS IT TRUE?


BAT BOY.                          PARKER.          SHELLEY.
   ALMOST ENOUGH TO
   SAVE ME …                                       … YES.
*(Sneering, to Parker.)*
   AND I IMAGINE YOU'RE
   "UPSET."                        OH MY *GOD* …
   BUT I WOULD *KILL* FOR
   HER AGAIN.
MOB.
   STOP HIM! KILL HIM!
BAT BOY.                                           ALL.
   AND DO YOU KNOW
   WHAT SHE DID THEN?                               STOP!
   SHE OFFERED ME HER VEIN,                         NO!
   SHE OFFERED ME HER BLOOD,                        GOD!
*(Roars.)*
   SHE OFFERED ME *EVERYTHING!*
*(With a roar, Parker throws the willing Bat Boy to the ground and raises the knife.
Meredith touches Parker. Their eyes meet. Long pause.)*
PARKER.                     MEREDITH.
   MEREDITH, I'M
   SORRY.

| | |
|---|---|
| ALL OF THIS IS ME.<br>I CAN'T BEAR<br>TO LOOK AT HIM.<br>YOU ARE ALL I SEE.<br>HIS EYES, MEREDITH,<br>HE HAS YOUR EYES.<br>IT HURTS TOO MUCH<br>TO PUT BEHIND ME ... | THOMAS, PLEASE.<br><br>THOMAS DON'T.<br>PLEASE, OH THOMAS,<br>DON'T DENY THE OBVIOUS,<br>LEAVE THE PAST BEHIND,<br>WE CAN START AGAIN, LOVE.<br>WE HAVE BOTH BEEN BLIND. |

MOB.

| | | |
|---|---|---|
| THE WAY I LOST<br>YOU.<br>AND EVERY DAY<br>HIS EYES<br>REMIND ME. | THOMAS,<br>I FORGIVE YOU ...<br>I KNOW, MY LOVE,<br>I KNOW ...<br>THOMAS, COME<br>HERE.<br>THOMAS, LET HIM<br>GO ... | PARKER,<br>DAMN YOU,<br>PARKER,<br>YOU DO IT<br>NOW ...<br>NOW!<br><br>NOW!<br>NOWWW!!! |

*(Parker turns to Bat Boy.)*

PARKER. Are you hungry, Edgar? *(Parker raises the knife — and cuts a gash in his own neck. It bleeds. Bat Boy can't resist the blood. He leaps at Parker and bites his neck. Parker raises the knife, stabs Bat Boy's back. Bat Boy now bites harder on Parker's neck. Parker raises the knife for another stab. Meredith grabs on to Bat Boy and tries to pull him off. Parker stabs down, now striking Meredith in the back. Hold on this embrace. They stagger. The dying takes some time. Finally, Parker and Meredith fall away from Bat Boy in unison. Bat Boy is left standing, wounded. Shelley runs to him. He falls. She cradles his head in her hands.)*

SHELLEY. Oh, Edgar. My dear sweet boy.

BAT BOY. I am not a boy. I am an animal. *(Bat Boy dies. Pause. The Institute Man, wearing a white uniform and carrying one of those animal-control leash poles, enters running.)*

INSTITUTE MAN. Where is this ... *(He takes in the carnage.)* Oh, God.

SHERIFF. You're late.

INSTITUTE MAN. What happened here?

SHERIFF. It's a long story. I don't know where to begin. *(Long pause. The towns-folk regard each other, shamed. Music. Shelley lifts her head and looks at the audience.)*

## "FINALE: HOLD ME, BAT BOY (REPRISE)"
### *(Shelley, Chorus)*

SHELLEY.
  IN A CAVE MANY MILES TO THE SOUTH
  LIVED A BOY BORN WITH FANGS IN HIS
  MOUTH.
  HE NEVER KNEW WHAT HE WAS WORTH;
  I COULD NOT STOP HIS FALL.
  YET IN HIS PRECIOUS HOURS ON EARTH
  HE TAUGHT US ALL.
MAGGIE.
  LOVE YOUR NEIGHBOR,
RICK.
  FORGIVE,
INSTITUTE MAN.
  KEEP YOUR VOWS.
BUD and NED.
  AND A MOUNTAIN'S NO PLACE TO RAISE COWS.
SHERIFF.
  REVENGE IS SOMETHING GOD FORBIDS,
BUD.
  TO SCAPEGOAT FOLKS IS WRONG.
RICK, RON and RUTHIE.
  AND DON'T KILL MRS. TAYLOR'S KIDS.
MEREDITH.
  LET GO THE FEARS TO WHICH YOU CLING,
MEREDITH and PARKER.
  AND THROUGH YOUR TEARS YOU'LL HEAR HIM
  SING,
MEREDITH, PARKER and SHELLEY.
  LIFT UP YOUR EARS AND JOIN HIS SONG!
MEREDITH, PARKER, SHELLEY and TOWNSFOLK.
  AND JOIN HIS SONG, AND JOIN HIS SONG,
  AND JOIN HIS SONG!
*(Bat Boy appears, standing and bloodied. He joins the chorus.)*

ALL.
    AH AH, AH AH, AH AH:
    HOLD YOUR BAT BOY,
    TOUCH YOUR BAT BOY.
    NO MORE NEED TO HIDE.
    KNOW YOUR BAT BOY,
    LOVE YOUR BAT BOY.
    DON'T DENY YOUR BEAST INSIDE!
    AH, AH,
    *AH!*

## END

# PROPERTY LIST

## ACT ONE

### Scene 1
Rappelling ropes and gear (3 sets)
3 miner's helmets with attached spotlights
Small bong (i.e., water pipe)
Lighter
Small bag of Fritos
Red wagon
Burlap sack

### Scenes 2 and 3
Sofa
Coffee table
2 chairs
Credenza
Furniture polish (2 cans)
2 dust rags
Handcuffs
Pistol
Cage
Whole, cooked chicken
Platter
Candles and holders
Bowie knife
Oven mitt
Matches
Pot of stew
Wooden spoon

### Scene 4
Bench
Podium
Gavel
Meat hooks
Notepad
Pen
Cell phone
Handkerchief

### Scene 5
Dead geese on string (one filled with blood)
Shotgun

Hunting knife
Candle
Doctor's bag
Liquor flask
Pocket tape recorder
Syringe
Vial
Martini glass
Cocktail shaker
Basin

**Scene 6**
Hospital bed or wheelchair
Clipboard (doctor's chart)
Pen

**Scene 7**
Sofa
Coffee table
2 chairs
Credenza
Children's book
Tea service
Rat
Flash cards (pictures optional)
Pictures (or slides)
Videocassettes
Records
Blue essay book

**Scene 8**
Gavel

**Scene 9**
Sofa
Coffee table
2 chairs
Credenza
Finger sandwiches
Tea service
Rabbit filled with blood
Ironing board
Iron
Sunday dress

## ACT TWO

### Scene 1
Podium with cross
Preacher's bible
Common bibles
Fans
Gun

### Scene 3
Handkerchief
Large leaves/small shrubs

### Scene 4
Torch
Walkie-talkie

### Scene 6
Cow's head
2 shotguns
Test tubes
Table on wheels
Bats on sticks
Baby Shelley
Bat baby
Bundle
Shovel
Handcuffs
Retractable knife filled with blood
Animal control leash pole